THE TURNING KEY

THE TURNING KEY

*Autobiography and the Subjective
Impulse since 1800*

***

Jerome Hamilton Buckley

HARVARD UNIVERSITY PRESS

Cambridge, Massachusetts, and London, England

1984

820.93
B924t
1984

This book is printed on acid-free paper, and its binding materials have been chosen for strength and durability.

Library of Congress Cataloging in Publication Data

Buckley, Jerome Hamilton.
    The turning key.

    Includes bibliographical references and index.
    1. English prose literature—History and criticism.
2. Autobiography. 3. Subjectivity in literature.
4. Self in literature. 5. Authors, English—Biography.
I. Title.
PR756.A9B8   1984   820'.9'353   83-13033
ISBN 0-674-91330-2

TO
MADELEINE DORAN
AND
SAN AND CARL WOODRING

PREFACE

Many recent studies of autobiography describe that elusive genre in current "new-critical" terms, linguistic, structuralist, or deconstructionist. Some alert us to the imprecision and ambiguity of all language of the self. Most, seeking to establish the integrity of the text as an independent artifact with its own deep structure, assume the "death" or absence or irrelevance of the author, or at least an essential difference between the printed life and any actual lived experience. Nearly all regard autobiography as a process of semifictional self-creation, with little or no necessary parallel to an extratextual fact or truth, but with some attention, nonetheless, to an "intertextuality," which offers patterns to imitate or reject and some common conventions of self-depiction.

The notes appended to the present book acknowledge my awareness of such criticism and at times my considerable indebtedness to it. Yet my own purpose and approach are somewhat different, for I am here concerned more with the function of autobiography than with a definition of its form. Though I should not wish to ignore the aesthetic dimension and impact of a self-history as a literary object in itself, I have chosen first of all to explore what I have called "the subjective impulse," the writer's assumption that he or she may or even must confess, explain, divulge, or simply display an innermost self to a putative audience.

Like other students of the genre, I recognize the place of St. Augustine in the autobiographical tradition, and I pause to pay tribute to his influence. But, again like others, I see a distinct difference—in intention, method, and quality of self-consciousness—between Augustine's *Confessions* in the fourth century and Rousseau's in the eighteenth, and I accept as essentially valid the claims of Rousseau and of Wordsworth a generation later that, in diverse ways, their extended self-revelations were indeed quite unprecedented. Though my second chapter glances at a few earlier subjective writings, this book as a whole concentrates attention on evidences from the period after 1800. In passing it considers a few American and Continental European autobiographers, but it draws mainly on the British and Irish writers with whom I am most familiar, especially those examining their spiritual or mental condition, from Wordsworth in *The Prelude* to Samuel Beckett in *Company*.

Since subjectivity expresses itself in several literary forms, I have considered at least briefly the autobiographical novel and the personal poem, as well as, more intently, the formal self-history. I have excluded the drama in the belief that the theatre, no matter how personal an instrument it becomes, conceals and to some degree objectifies through dialogue any subjective intention the playwright may have had. My primary focus, at all events, is directed toward the sustained and ostensibly nonfictional autobiography as the least mediated demonstration of the working sanctions behind self-scrutiny and self-revelation. It should soon be apparent that I regard egregious subjectivity with some misgiving, that I see dangers as well as advantages in a prolonged self-contemplation, and that I value the autobiography that opens the door from a private sensibility to a general psychology, above that which locks the individual in upon his solitary self. From the perspective I have adopted, Wordsworth's assertion of the "ordinary" grounds of vision seems to me perpetually pertinent. At its most vital, the literature of the self, I should think, must be more than self-reflexive.

The time-span of this book, from about 1800 onwards, also saw the unprecedented emergence of women writers, especially after the Romantic period, as major forces in English literature. But there have been remarkably few women autobiographers devoted intensely, like Wordsworth or Ruskin or Edwin Muir, to the projection of their inner lives, and I note the virtual absence of women from my general argument. A number of women, of course, have written cogently of their careers and special interests. Mrs. Oliphant and Mrs. Humphry Ward, for example, compiled revealing records of their struggles and successes as professional authors. Harriet Martineau and Beatrice Webb as committed sociologists strove to place their personal reminiscences in the wider context of social history. Emmeline Pankhurst in *My Own Story* told less of herself than of a passionate crusade and every woman's need for self-assertion. And Vera Brittain testified poignantly, from personal witness, to the growth of a pacifist conviction in a madly belligerent world. Nonetheless, the more private subjective impulse in women writers seems for the most part to have been better satisfied in autobiographical fiction—such as that of Dorothy Richardson or Doris Lessing—than in non-fictional personal narrative. In any case, as we move into the later twentieth century, the subjective novel, which demands a certain distancing from single-minded self-scrutiny, has tended among all writers, both male and female, to displace the more direct spiritual autobiography.

Some preliminary reading for this study was completed

in California, during a sabbatical leave, on a Huntington Library Fellowship. Parts of several chapters were delivered as papers to the Harvard Victorians and as guest lectures at New York University, Ottawa and Queen's in Canada, the Virginia Polytechnic Institute and State University, and the International Association of University Professors of English meeting in Hamburg, West Germany. Chapter V in somewhat altered form appears in *Modernism Reconsidered*, ed. Robert Kiely (Cambridge, Mass.: Harvard University Press, 1983). I am grateful to all these institutions and groups for providing assistance, audience, and encouragement. I have also benefited from the helpful advice of many students and colleagues; I must especially thank David Staines, Peter Dale, Donald D. Stone, James Engell, Brooke Hopkins, Deborah Nord, George P. Landow, and Robert Folkenflik for their expressed interest in my theme. I am indebted to Victoria Macy for help in preparing my manuscript and to Anita Safran for a number of editorial suggestions. And as always I appreciate the sympathy and patience of my wife, Elizabeth. Finally I dedicate this short monograph to three friends of long acquaintance, the thought of whom, as it would in any autobiography, steadily brings the light of other days around me.

J.H.B.

Cambridge, Massachusetts
September 1983

CONTENTS

THE TURNING KEY

≈§ I ≥≈

THE UNPRECEDENTED SELF

It will . . . be . . . a thing unprecedented in Literary history that a man should talk so much about himself.

—Wordsworth, 1805

W ITH a skeptical impatience and a reluctant respect Carlyle pictured Coleridge as the sage of Highgate, the table-talker, deep in German metaphysics, snuffling in a hypnotic sing-song of "om-m-mject" and "sum-m-mject." These terms, Carlyle explained, were "of continual recurrence in the Kantean province,"[1] but nonetheless to English ears, in Coleridge's time, new, surprising, and abstruse.

The words "objective" and "subjective" had of course entered the language long before the advent of European idealism. But they had little currency in nineteenth-century England until Coleridge, as he himself put it, "ventured to re-introduce" them as convenient descriptions of the perceived and the perceiver in the new philosophy.[2] They accordingly appeared to such purpose in his *Biographia Literaria* of 1817 and in his essays on method in *The Friend*, and eventually "subjective" acquired broader applications.

At the time of his late table talk Coleridge was much concerned with the "subjective" element in poetry. There he identified two kinds of subjectivity: an author's writing of his own emotion and an author's presentation of dramatic

1

characters engaged in introspection and self-analysis. Milton and Shakespeare, he said, illustrated the difference: "There is a subjectivity of the poet, as of Milton, who is himself before himself in every thing he writes; and there is a subjectivity of the *persona*, . . . as in all Shakespeare's great creations," especially Hamlet and Lear, but Shakespeare's work is otherwise objective, "characterless—that is, it does not reflect the individual Shakespeare."[3] Modern poetry, he concluded, was, for better or worse, obviously closer to the Miltonic mode.

By 1840, six years after Coleridge's death, the term "subjective" was still new but no longer strange, for as Edward FitzGerald wrote to Frederick Tennyson in Italy, "This word has made considerable progress in England during the year you have been away, so that people begin to fancy they understand what it means. I have been striving at it, because it is a very *sine qua non* condition in a book which I have just been reading." FitzGerald apparently understood its meaning well enough eventually to urge Frederick to publish his highly subjective verses ("your own genuine reflex of *you*"): "The whole *subjective* scheme (damn the word!) of the poems I did not like; but that is quite a genuine mould of your soul . . ."[4] Thus, despite his distaste for the term and its referent, FitzGerald could not escape the label, nor wholly deny the claims of a subjective poetry.

Throughout the nineteenth century "subjective" became a more and more familiar critical counter, and among the later Victorians talk of subjective and objective matters, often remote from Kantian epistemology, had become popular jargon—as we may gather from the quite literary lament of Ralph Rackstraw in *H.M.S. Pinafore*:

In me there meet a combination of antithetical elements which are at eternal war with one another. Driven hither by objective influences—

thither by subjective emotions—wafted one moment into blazing day, by mocking hope—plunged the next into Cimmerian darkness of tangible despair, I am but a living ganglion of irreconcilable antagonisms. I hope I make myself clear, lady?[5]

Small wonder that Josephine, the captain's daughter, responds in an aside, "His simple eloquence goes to my heart." For Ralph has caught the idiom of his time.

Though it did not invent subjectivity (neither the word nor the condition it connotes), the nineteenth century was certainly the first period to speak self-consciously of the self as a major source of literary material, and the first, beginning with the Romantics, to write a great deal subjectively—that is, as Coleridge suggested, either of the self directly or of psychological states and values understood by self-contemplation. In 1805 when he completed the first full version of *The Prelude*—in some eight thousand lines—Wordsworth, forgetting for the moment the example of Rousseau, declared it "a thing unprecedented in literary history that a man should talk so much about himself."[6] But the precedent was freely imitated long before *The Prelude* was published in 1850. Hazlitt's judgment of Wordsworth's apparently subjective shorter poems was early and largely accurate: "He is the greatest, that is, the most original poet of the present day, only because he is the greatest egotist. . . . He does not waste a thought on others. Whatever does not relate exclusively and wholly to himself, is foreign to his views. . . . The object is nothing but as it furnishes food for internal meditations, for old associations."[7] *The Prelude*, most of us, I suppose, would now agree, is the most original and probably the greatest poem of Romantic England, and it remains, however we appraise it, the most considerable and conspicuous expression in poetry of the subjective impulse that has dominated much of modern culture.

In our time Erik Erikson, describing the crises of identity, speaks of "the newness of man's self-awareness and of his attention to his awareness," which has "led to a scientific mythology of the mind."[8] Such self-consciousness, however, is new only in relation to a long human history. It was already well established and rapidly increasing in the mid nineteenth century, and the spread of the epithet "subjective" was simply a symptom of its prevalence. Emerson indeed considered subjectivity the central attribute of the age. "The key to the period," he wrote near the end of his life, "seemed to be that the mind had become aware of itself. . . . There was a new consciousness. . . . The young men were born with knives in their brain, a tendency to introversion, self-dissection, anatomizing of motives."[9]

As one of the most sensitive of those sharp-edged young men, Gerard Manley Hopkins coined the verb "selve" to denote the action of discovering and proclaiming one's identity, the idiosyncratic difference of each individual life:

> Each mortal thing does one thing and the same:
>   Deals out that being indoors each one dwells;
>   Selves—goes itself; *myself* it speaks and spells,
> Crying *What I do is me: for that I came.*[10]

Again, in a prose meditation, Hopkins reflected on the peculiar intensity of his own "selfbeing," "my consciousness and feeling of myself, that taste of myself, of *I* and *me* above and in all things, which is more distinctive than the smell of walnutleaf or camphor, and is incommunicable by any means to another man (as when I was a child I used to ask myself: What must it be to be someone else?). Nothing else in nature comes near this unspeakable stress of pitch, distinctiveness, and selving, this selfbeing of my own."[11] But if he celebrated the unique inscape of self, Hopkins also recognized, with increasing insistence, as in the late "terrible sonnets," the tyranny of self-awareness, the bitterness of the taste, the souring "selfyeast of spirit."

Walter Pater, who had been Hopkins's tutor at Oxford, likewise saw the danger of an excessively introspective literature, where "imprisoned . . . in the narrow cell of its subjective experience, the action of a powerful nature will be intense, but exclusive and peculiar,"[12] distorting both the aesthetic form and any adequate perspective on content. But he was, nonetheless, in frequent sympathy with the subjective impulse, which he believed characteristic of the "modern" temper. In the essays of Charles Lamb he discerned with evident approval "the desire of self-portraiture" (another term of nineteenth-century invention), "below all more superficial tendencies," as "the real motive in writing at all—a desire closely connected with that intimacy, that modern subjectivity, which may be called the *Montaignesque* element in literature."[13] And in his Roman novel, *Marius the Epicurean*, he permitted his sensitive hero the "modernism" of keeping a private journal—a practice "seemingly rare among the ancients," who seldom, he said, afforded us "so much as a glimpse of that interior self, which in many cases would have actually doubled the interest of their objective informations."[14]

Oscar Wilde, as was his custom, went further. Though Pater's avowed disciple, he denied objectivity even to the ancient epic poets and to the Elizabethan dramatists, since all art, he declared (or rather had his *persona* Gilbert in *Intentions* declare for him), "All artistic creation is absolutely subjective." Thus the apparently objective Shakespeare expressed his inmost self through his protagonists: "Hamlet came out of his soul, and Romeo out of his passion."[15] The masks of art allowed Shakespeare to tell the whole truth about himself, just as various masks displayed yet protected the real Oscar Wilde, who confessed, perhaps truthfully, to living in constant fear of not being misunderstood.

In the twentieth century literary subjectivity has had a dubious reputation and a pervasive influence. A recent academic critic is persuaded that "the poet's own selfhood" must be the only true theme of modern poetry. T. S. Eliot, on the other hand, the great exemplar of the high modernist mode, liked to insist on the "objective correlative" as the necessary means of distancing poem from poet and so giving it aesthetic independence. But the disparity between the two views may be more apparent than real. For even to speak of an objective correlative is to imply that there is a subjective counterpart, the author's state of mind or emotion which requires dramatic embodiment. Both views reflect the common assumption that literature may, or indeed must, somehow be shaped from the writer's private experience, from the very heart of his inmost being. Eliot himself sensed only too keenly the restriction of self-consciousness. Near the end of *The Waste Land* he described the key locking each of us in the prison cell of self, and in an endnote to the poem he gave the notion its familiar sanction in idealist philosophy—he quoted from F. H. Bradley's *Appearance and Reality*, a book crucial in his own development:

My external sensations are no less private to myself than are my thoughts or my feelings. In either case my experience falls within my own circle, a circle closed on the outside; and, with all its elements alike, every sphere is opaque to the others which surround it. . . . In brief, regarded as an existence which appears in a soul, the whole world for each is peculiar and private to that soul.[16]

We must remind ourselves, nevertheless, that the assumption of subjectivity was by no means general before the Romantic period. Even among the major Romantics, Byron, at least in his masterpiece *Don Juan*, which is by many standards a most personal poem, kept a strong hold on objective social realities not to be grasped by self-analysis; and Keats, whose odes surely image something of his own intense struggle to preserve life and sanity, maintained that poets properly had no character, no individual identities, but exercised a "negative capability," and so existed only in and through the objects they had observed or imagined.

Few before 1800 would have accepted Coleridge's judgment that *Paradise Lost* is essentially a subjective revelation, and most readers would have regarded *Samson Agonistes*, despite a possible parallel between the blind hero and the poet, as a quite impersonal tragedy. Wilde's opinion to the contrary, we have no warrant to consider Romeo the mouthpiece of Shakespeare's passion or a wish fulfillment born of his frustration; nor have we good reason to believe Hamlet a reflection of his intellectual turmoil and indecision. In their fictions Defoe and Fielding, we may suppose, were less addicted to *self*-expression than Joyce or D. H. Lawrence. Similarly Jane Austen remains a relatively aloof ironic presence behind her novels, a restrained remote self, whereas Virginia Woolf appears as a diffusive sensibility, informing the collective consciousness of all her characters. In each instance, of course, we know far more of the private lives of the later writers. An indefatigable Virginia Woolf industry has provided us reams of documentation; in addition to detailed biographies, we have diaries, letters, notes, and journals, day-by-day accounts of over twenty years of the Woolfs' married life, and supplementary memoirs by relatives and other members of the Bloomsbury group. Our estimate of modern work is, rightly or wrongly, often conditioned by the degree of our intimacy with the writer

outside the text and by our taking for granted that his or
her "real motive in writing at all" was in some sort a conscious self-depiction.

Not all readers, however, have been willing to accept the
premise of subjective authorship. The New Critics of the
earlier twentieth century earnestly strove to detach art from
artist, to trust the tale rather than the teller, to appraise the
poem or story as an artifact beyond place and time. They
accordingly turned their talent and ingenuity to the expli-
cation of image, the analysis of tropes, rhythm, and rhetorical proportion, to the presence of paradox, irony, and
intrinsic ambiguities. And in so doing they recalled us to
the fact that, whatever the sources of a literary work, its
realized integrity as an object in itself determines much of
its quality and enduring impact. But in their formalism they
too often forgot that a poem could mean as well as be—
and mean in a larger comparative context; that poetry and
prose are to a degree less pure and self-sufficient than, say,
music, insofar as words are immediately referential, sometimes with local and private connotations, and that some
images may be wholly intelligible only within the frame of
the author's individual experience.

The recent heirs of the New Critics are less impatient
with meanings, and those who have appropriated and secularized the science of Scriptural interpretation known as
hermeneutics are intent on discovering the hidden implications of the literary narrative or structure. But they are
not the less eager to deny the relevance of a subjective origin.
Roland Barthes and the structuralists who follow his teach-
ings have proclaimed "the death of the author" and the
autonomous life of his creation. To Barthes all "author-
based" criticism is aesthetically false—and also politically
suspect, implying a business transaction, and the capitalist's

continuing stake in his literary property. The liberated poem now becomes an independent linguistic arrangement, not a memorial to the poet's personal experience or a correlative to any emotion recollected in tranquillity. The poet's single role now seems analogous to the dancer's; it coincides exactly with his performance; it neither precedes the exercise nor remains after it is over.

Yet the structuralists and the hermeneutic interpreters are scarcely more objective than the "author-based" critics they dismiss, for their "reader-based" analyses are frankly, and often defiantly, arbitrary and relativistic. The "hermeneutists" dissect the work without regard for the author's possible or declared intention but with their own "pre-understanding" of the aesthetic whole, and their readings of a given text may differ as sharply as their individual preparations and predispositions. If they ignore or repudiate the subjective author, they affirm, in their own new jargon, the subjectivity of the critic.[17] And so, deliberately or inadvertently, they reinstate the authority of Oscar Wilde, who, far more engagingly than his latest disciples, had his paradoxical Gilbert describe criticism at its best as "the purest form of personal expression, . . . in its way more creative than creation, as it has the least reference to any standard external to itself. . . . It is the only civilized form of autobiography, as it deals not with the events but with the thoughts of one's life. . . . [It] is in its essence purely subjective, and seeks to reveal its own secret, and not the secret of another. For the highest Criticism deals with art not as expressive but as impressive purely."[18]

Both the author who turns to his inward experience and the critic who finds the necessity of a private and esoteric reading have long since assumed some radical disjunction between art and society. Whether or not he came out of

Shakespeare's soul, as Wilde suggested, Hamlet has seemed
to many, from the time of the Romantics onward, the archetypal subjective hero, disaffected, alienated by his own
acute perceptions, brooding on the injustices of an outrageous fortune. This hypersensitive Hamlet (for there are of
course other approaches to the character) is the troubled
soul identified by Coleridge as one to whom "the external
world, and all its incidents and objects were comparatively
dim, and of no interest in themselves, and which began to
interest only when they were reflected in the mirror of his
mind."[19] Matthew Arnold saw in Hamlet an early example
of the modern "dialogue of the mind with itself"[20] and as
such, even though the creation of the greatest of poets, a
regrettable lapse from the cheerful objectivity of the ancients. Walter Bagehot, who had similar misgivings about
subjective poetry, contended that the value of *Hamlet* as a
play could not depend on the qualities of the ambivalent
hero, since "the internal metaphysics of a divided nature
are but an inferior subject for art, and if they are to be
made attractive, much else must be combined with them."
And in another context he adjudged Coleridge's subjective
verses in terms strikingly like the poet's description of Hamlet's malady:

In fact, it would appear that the tendency to, and the faculty for, self-
delineation, are very closely connected with the dreaminess of disposition
and impotence of character which we spoke of just now. Persons very
subject to these can grasp no external object, comprehend no external
being; they can do no external thing, and therefore they are left to
themselves. Their own character is the only one which they can view
as a whole, or depict as a reality. . . .[21]

In the "American Scholar" address of 1837 Emerson had
sought to rally desponding intellectuals of "the age of In-

troversion, . . . infected with Hamlet's unhappiness,—
'Sicklied o'er with the pale cast of thought.' " Sixty years
later, speaking of and for the late Victorians, "Mark Rutherford" quoted the same line as a fitting description of his
sad self-questioning contemporaries.[22] By the early twentieth century introspection, self-analysis, self-delineation,
and the divided mind were thoroughly established as ways
of life and literature. D. H. Lawrence, for one, accepted
"the self-tortured Hamlet" as representative of "our sort of
subjective consciousness," but, however much he deplored
in general the self-absorption of others, he respected, and
indeed encouraged, his own inner debate. He denied neither
the uneasy voice within, "the skeleton in the cupboard of
[his] inside," nor a will to sustain the dialogue: "And what
should I do without him? No, no, I'm quite at home with
my good and bony skeleton. So he wants to have a chat
with me, let him."[23] And more than a little of the internal
colloquy carried over into Lawrence's published work.

The disaffected modern man readily finds reasons for
withdrawal and alienation undreamt of in Hamlet's philosophy. Popular culture, while demanding stereotypes and
interchangeable parts, unwittingly provides abundant in-
centive for rebellion and nonconformity. The intellectual
in our time, especially the artist, regards as truisms the
bleakest of premises. The plural society is necessarily atom-
istic; the division of labor and ever-increasing specialization
have raised barriers against shared activity and free communication and set a premium on individual performance.
Each of us proves himself by asserting his uniqueness, and
the "subjective consciousness," shut off from the larger world,
alone guarantees our difference. The private person becomes more important than the social being, and personal
intuition or even prejudice outweighs reliance on a consen-

sus of rational opinion, with the result that all sense of a general normative response begins to fade and vanish. Politics, the life of public service, insofar as it is manipulated by mass media and involves constant compromise of standards, proves less and less attractive to the independent thinker. Above all—perhaps the most efficient cause of disaffection—the decline of religious authority, in almost every earlier civilization the prime guardian of public morals, has left many to cope in bewilderment with a situational ethics, which receives no apparent sanction from a vast indifferent universe.

Bertrand Russell argued that, with the loss of religion, "human comradeship seems to grow more intimate and more tender from the sense that we are all exiles on an inhospitable shore,"[24] just as Arnold, a century earlier, suggested that the ebbing of the sea of faith made it all the more necessary for the lovers, left stranded on the darkling plain, to be true to one another. Arnold, however, recognized that even in love the moments of complete understanding—or, at any rate, of the illusion of real insight into life's purposes—were rare and transitory. If therefore an individual could not for long share the whole truth with another, he must learn to be true to himself, must cultivate an uncomplaining Arnoldian "self-dependence." Though it no longer commanded the old allegiance, religion, especially in its Christian and Protestant form, had left to the doubters and agnostics of Arnold's time and later the habit of introspection and the appeal to private conscience. The young John Stuart Mill, though trained in a narrow rationalism, found salvation of sorts in self-questioning, which led to the discovery of the neglected imagination and its pleasures and so to the eventual qualitative enrichment of a naive Benthamism. Other Victorians and early moderns turned to

personal values (whatever sanction they might have) in reaction to the cold objectivities of natural science. When the
primary meaning of "nature" was no longer "human nature," the lonely self, like the "soul" of the old religion, had
to seek the vital reasons of the heart which scientific reason
could not know.

But the self invoked by the Romantics and their succes-
sors is hardly the same self that Pope had in mind when he
repeated the counsel of the oracle at Delphi:

> Know then thyself, presume not God to scan;
> The proper study of mankind is man.

The self to Pope was general, a stable entity representative
of all mankind, a sort of common consciousness, and not
an idiosyncratic private possession. It retained something
of this generality as late as Cardinal Newman, who spoke
of "self-knowledge" as the source of man's understanding
of God, "at the root of all real religious knowledge," for "it
is in proportion as we search our hearts and understand our
own nature, that we understand what is meant by an Infinite
Governor and Judge."[25] But such assumptions about a common human nature were becoming increasingly rare in
Newman's time. By the end of the eighteenth century the
personal, fluid, individual self, or rather the many separate
selves and "dead selves" of each man, distinct from all others, had begun to replace the fixed and average public self.
The great self-possessed Goethe, in awe no doubt of his
own inner mystery, claimed he could not know himself—
"and God forbid that I should."[26] Coleridge similarly, in a
late poem entitled "Self-Knowledge," self-consciously in-
verted Pope's exhortation: Know thyself? "What is there in
thee, Man, that can be known?" For the self is now simply

"Dark fluxion, all unfixable by thought." Coleridge's admonition accordingly becomes, "Ignore thyself, and strive to know thy God!" Yet the self was not readily to be ignored, least of all by the interpreter of "subjectivity," and God often seemed available or knowable only through personal intuition.

In late eighteenth-century English literature the accent falls less and less on the type and ever more insistently on the individual. The novel, especially the work of Sterne, devoted to particulars, offers a gallery of eccentrics, whose conduct may image the peculiar foibles of the presiding novelist.[27] And biography, following Boswell's conspicuous example, moves from the depiction of general human nature to the portrayal of distinctive personality. At the same time the voice of the individual poet begins to break through the decorous anonymity of neoclassical verse. Burns sings of his own sentiments and sorrows; Blake develops his private mythology and declares in his own generalization that "to generalize is to be an idiot." Less aggressively new, indeed in many respects a traditionalist, Cowper, in "The Castaway" of 1799, tells a rather conventional and apparently quite objective tale of a sailor lost at sea and then suddenly, in the eleventh and final stanza, perhaps the last lines he ever wrote, unexpectedly gives the narrative a deeply personal application:

> No voice divine the storm allayed,
>   No light propitious shone,
> When, snatched from all effectual aid,
>   We perished, each alone;
> But I beneath a rougher sea,
> And whelmed in deeper gulfs than he.[28]

The drowning of the sailor has become an image of the poet's damnation; the subjective note has taken over, and the reader is left thinking not of the lost seaman but of Cowper himself in lonely despair and madness.

The shift toward a more subjective poetry was symptomatic of a wider change throughout society from the 1760s onwards. It now seems reasonable to assume that the modern self was "invented shortly after the middle of the eighteenth century."[29] "Imagined" is perhaps a more accurate word than "invented," for invention implies the discovery or production of a real object, whereas to the philosopher the new self is a fiction, a convenient working hypothesis, rather than a fact to be measured and described. In an increasingly secular world "self" has become a euphemism or substitute of "soul." But there were from the beginning marked differences between the two concepts; the soul was fixed and immortal, lent to man by God, and returning after an earthly span to its divine source; the self, on the other hand, was transitory, coterminous with the physical body, simply the sum of the individual's sensations at any given moment. Locke, though a religious man, had weakened the concept of the soul by denying the presence of innate ideas, a priori knowledge, and all intimations of a preexistence. Hume argued more explicitly that the soul did not exist apart from its perceptions, that soul or mind— or self—was indeed but a bundle of impressions and associations, not a substance but a function of consciousness. Finally to Kant, who affirmed and then greatly modified Hume's skepticism, our knowledge of all essential realities, of "things-in-themselves," was relative and imperfect, and the realm of practical morals, neither to be proven nor disproven by science, yet of the highest urgency, was subjectively contingent, available only to the elusive perceiving and relating self.

By the time of Wordsworth the self was not so much Hume's bundle of present perceptions as the remembrance of past impressions and ideas; the "I" was, first of all, what "I" remembered. The self thus acquired a continuity beyond the constant flux of sensation. Tennyson in *In Memoriam* reflected current opinion associating memory and self when he described the infant's acquisition of a distinct individuality:

> So rounds he to a separate mind
>   From whence clear memory may begin,
>   As thro' the frame that binds him in
> His isolation grows defined.

The Victorian psychologist Alexander Bain identified all consciousness with memory in the belief that we were not actually conscious of a fact unless we could remember it immediately afterwards.[30] John Stuart Mill agreed in principle: "I see no reason," he said, "to think that there is any cognizance of an Ego until Memory commences." He was convinced that "the theory . . . which resolves Mind into a series of feelings" could withstand any contrary argument. Nonetheless, he found difficulties in the theory "beyond the power of metaphysical analysis to remove." If the mind or self was a series of feelings, it was also "aware of itself as past and future"; could a series of feelings, he wondered, ever be aware of itself as a series? But if there were problems in regarding mind merely as function rather than as substance, "Memory and Expectation," he insisted, still had "no equivalent in matter." Yet memory was the very core of selfhood: "remembering that it has been felt before is the simplest and most elementary fact of memory: and the inexplicable tie or law, . . . which connects the present consciousness with the past one, of which it reminds me, is as near as I think we can get to a positive conception of Self."[31]

Impatient with such speculation, Carlyle was prepared to accept Memory and Hope as "mystic faculties," never to be wholly understood, and to recognize, as the producer—or was it the product?—of both, "a certain inarticulate Self-consciousness" dwelling dimly within, "which only our Works can render articulate and decisively discernible." Like Coleridge, he found the precept *Know thyself* essentially "impossible"—at least "till it be translated into this partially possible one, *Know what thou canst work at.*" Carlyle's counsel of self-denial or renunciation—or *Selbst-tödtung* or *Entsagen* or whatever Diogenes Teufelsdröckh in *Sartor Resartus* cares to call it—does not mean, as some readers have alleged, his denial that there actually is a self; it implies rather that the peremptory self, very much a fact of experience, can be apprehended or realized not in introspection but, paradoxically, only in selfless thought and action. Intrinsically a mystery beyond definition and physical measurement, the Carlylean self, the "ME," resembles the more orthodox soul, at least in its divine origin, and it expresses its spirituality in resisting the menace of materialism: "Thus had the Everlasting No (*das ewige Nein*) pealed authoritatively through all the recesses of my Being, of my ME; and then it was that my whole ME stood up, in native God-created majesty, and with emphasis recorded its Protest."[32]

Carlyle both attacked and defended the subjective impulse. Undue attention to the inner life, he admitted, might lead in some eras to superstition and fanaticism, and self-absorbed withdrawal at any time could be disastrous. But the danger in the Mechanical Age, which was the nineteenth century as he saw it, lay in the opposite direction, in the repudiation of creative thought and passion, the "Dynamical" world of the spirit, which should engage "the primary, unmodified forms and energies of man."[33] Accordingly, as biographer and historian, he strove to extol the lives of great men who had been able to express the dynamics of vigorous selfhood, and in so doing he placed great value on "auto-biography," the personal records of his heroes. He praised Goethe's *Dichtung und Wahrheit* for accomplishing "the difficult problem of Autobiography with what seems a singular success." What would we not give, he asked, for "an Autobiography of Shakespeare"? Teufelsdröckh appears repeatedly as "our Autobiographer" and speaks to us by ironic indirection from "the Autobiographical Chaos" of his prose remains. Indeed in Weissnichtwo, as in many of Carlyle's histories, "the whole conversation is little or nothing else but Biography or Auto-Biography."[34]

If *Sartor Resartus* did not introduce the term, "autobiography" was still a comparatively new word in the 1830s, and Carlyle, always ready for semantic experiment, eagerly rang changes upon it. The word seems to have made its first appearance shortly after Carlyle's birth in 1795, but it was not well established until the early Victorian period. The once popular children's riddle, "Who wrote *The Autobiography of Benjamin Franklin?*" has, properly speaking, an unexpected answer: "Certainly not Benjamin Franklin—at least not under that title." For "The Memoirs of my Life" that Franklin left behind unfinished was first published as *The Autobiography* in 1868,[35] and the word itself was, as far as I can determine, quite unknown at the time of Franklin's death in 1790. Seven years later, doing an anonymous review of Isaac D'Israeli's *Miscellanies*, a journalist, probably William Taylor of Norwich, called attention to the antiquarian's discussion of "self-biography": "It is not very usual in English to employ hybrid words partly Saxon and partly Greek: yet *autobiography* would have seemed pedantic."[36] We cannot tell from the context whether some more pedantic writer had already coined the word, or whether the reviewer himself was simply trying to imagine for the occasion a neologism with consistent Greek roots. Apparently content with the hybrid, Coleridge in 1804 praised an early draft of *The Prelude* as Wordsworth's "divine Self-biography." But by 1809 his friend Robert Southey was using "auto-biography"—without embarrassment, yet with a hyphen—to describe the work of the Portuguese poet Francisco Vieira.[37] And by the time of Carlyle's early essays the term and its derivatives were becoming familiar in the quarterlies.

Pedantic-sounding or not to the first innocent ears, "autobiography" arose to satisfy a rapidly growing need. Like "subjectivity" it entered a new vocabulary for a new concern with selfhood and self-expression. As a practice, autobiography is one of the major genres of modern literature, and autobiographical elements impinge freely upon modern fiction and poetry. But its modern form began to emerge only with the eighteenth-century "invention" of the self, perhaps little more than a generation before the term. A careful survey has recovered only twenty-three autobiographies, some indeed quite slight, written by British men of letters in all the years before 1800, and then in the nineteenth century alone at least one hundred and seventy-five, most of which are decidedly different in kind from their predecessors.[38] Such an increase is not to be accounted for entirely or even primarily by the growth of population or the spread of literacy, which opened new opportunities to the writer. It is an index, rather, of a more profound change, of the rise of self-consciousness throughout society and of a new reverence for the subjective impulse in literature. More persistently than Coleridge could have imagined, the "subject" in both art and life became the principal "object" of attention and regard.

❧ II ❧

TOWARDS AUTOBIOGRAPHY

Je forme une entreprise qui n'eut jamais d'exemple,
et qui n'aurait point d'imitateur. Je veux montrer
à mes semblables un homme dans toute la vérité
de la nature; et cet homme, ce sera moi.

—*Jean-Jacques Rousseau*

As Matthew Arnold imputed to Empedocles a quite Victorian malaise, so Jacques Lacan, drawing on the same legend, assigns to him a Freudian and modern death-urge.[1] Empedocles, he writes, "by throwing himself into Mount Etna, leaves forever present in the memory of men this symbolic act of his being-for-death." Thus construed, the Greek philosopher's last gesture becomes a personal statement of a kind extremely rare at a time when suicide was decidedly more common than public testimony of alienation. Though self-doubt, ambivalence of emotion, and perverse desire were surely not unknown in classical culture, the most determined effort has gathered little evidence of any strong subjective impulse at work in Greek or Roman literature.[2] The *Confessions* of St. Augustine, compelling in many respects, is all the more remarkable for its uniqueness as the archetypal spiritual autobiography. In depth of self-analysis and scope of intimate revelation, it clearly transcends all documents before it in the ancient world and far surpasses all that follow for twelve hundred years in medieval and Renaissance Europe.

Early in the account of his delinquencies Augustine pauses self-consciously to explain—to himself and others, but not to God, who requires no explanation—his motives in confessing:

> To whom do I tell these things? Not to you, my God, but before you I tell them to my own kind, to mankind, or to whatever small part of it may come upon these books of mine. Why do I tell these things? It is that I myself and whoever else reads them may realize from what great depths we must cry unto you.[3]

Augustine never loses sight of his didactic purpose. Confession is good for his soul (and for the souls of others)—the soul that lives before and after the body and that, once free of the accidents of the flesh, loses the attributes of a private idiosyncratic self. Though he confesses unsparingly, he never seeks to gratify the ego; unlike many later self-revealers, he takes no pride in his sin. The lust of adolescence and the debauchery of early manhood, though the source of fearful remorse to him, are less vivid in terms of circumstantial data than the despoiling of the pear tree, which most autobiographers would consider a comparatively venial offense. But even this most memorable episode is quickly and simply recounted. Here, as constantly throughout the *Confessions*, the action is significant only for the reaction it evokes. The theft of the pears stands in retrospect not as a boyish prank but as a deliberate act of the perverse will, a trespass planned and executed in bad company and so a conspiracy of evil. As he broods over successive transgressions with a subtle psychology, a guilt quickened by an unforgotten pleasure in wrong-doing, Augustine relates each outward experience to the development of his inner life, until his book as a whole becomes an intense Bildungsroman. The climax of his self-observed growth comes with his reading of a passage from *Romans* in a garden at Milan and his conversion, long prepared for and reluctantly deferred, but at the last sudden and complete: "Instantly, in truth, at the end of this sentence, as if before a peaceful light streaming into my heart, all the dark shadows of doubt fled away."[4] The moment of vision, the "epiphany," is wholly spiritual, without sensuous dimension; yet the imagination of the engaged reader readily supplies the essential details of its physical setting.

To Augustine the "passions of the mind," desire, sadness, fear, and especially joy, are more vivid than the life of sensations—and more memorable: "I never," he writes, "saw, or heard, or smelled, or tasted, or touched joy by a bodily sense. I have experienced it in my mind, when I have rejoiced, and knowledge of it has clung to my memory."[5] Here, as in many later autobiographies, "mind" and "memory" are virtually synonymous terms, and memory as a faculty is of inestimable value. Augustine, generalizing from his own particular impressions and responses, becomes a preeminent philosopher of memory. No autobiographer has ever described the actual processes of recollection with greater diligence and depth. None has reflected with comparable wonder, in many images, on the meaning of memory and its involutions, its variety and selectivity, and the persistence of its operation, as if the remembering, often beyond voluntary control, were the very essence of living:

I come into the fields and spacious palaces of my memory, where are treasures of countless images of things of every manner, brought there from objects perceived by sense. . . .

The great cave of memory, and I know not what hidden and inexpressible recesses within it, takes in all these things to be called up and brought forth when there is need for them. . . .

These acts I perform within myself in the vast court of my memory. Within it are present to me sky, earth, and sea, together with all things that I could perceive in them, aside from all the things I have forgotten. There too I encounter myself and recall myself, and what, and when, and where I did some deed, and how I was affected when I did it. . . .

Great is the power of memory, exceeding great is it, O God, an inner chamber, vast and unbounded! Who has penetrated to its very bottom? Yet it is a power of my mind and it belongs to my nature, and thus I do not comprehend all that I am. Is the mind, therefore, too limited to possess itself? Must we ask, "Where is this power belonging to it which it does not grasp?" "Is it outside it, and not within it?" "How then does it not comprehend it?" Great wonder arises within me at this. Amazement seizes me. . . .

Great is the power of memory! An awesome thing, my God, deep and boundless and manifold in being! And this thing is the mind, and this am I myself: What then am I, O my God? What is my nature? A life varied and manifold and mightily surpassing measurement.[6]

Memory functions in time, and Augustine ponders the mysteries of time with a similar profundity and precision: is the past real? is the future? or is there only a now so instantaneous that it cannot be detected before it is already the past? Time so regarded is constant flux in linear progression. Though able to remember and record moments of crisis and revelation, Augustine has comparatively little to say of qualitative time, of how and why some intervals seem to the self living through them longer, more intense, and more significant than others. He is deeply preoccupied with the eternity to which the liberated soul belongs and eventually returns. But the concept of a this-worldly duration as a kind of secular foretaste of the eternal does not concern him. And it does not become a decisive force in autobiography until many centuries after his death, not indeed until the Romantics began exploring anew the tortuous paths of subjectivity.

The *Confessions*, however wide its ultimate influence on more secular thought, was of course first of all a major essay in Christian apologetics, relating directly to a tradition of narratives of conversion and dedication. Subjective writing with a like intent, as it reappeared at intervals, notably in the twelfth century, involved the stripping away of individual personality in the effort to bare an inner self, less idiosyncratic, more general, and closer to the spirit of God.[7] This process, repeated throughout the Middle Ages and on into the Reformation, demanded and evolved subtle techniques of introspection and refined analysis of the suffering soul as it sought to deny and then to recognize and finally to transcend the burden of original sin. In the troubled ambience of seventeenth-century England when religious uncertainty and civil strife called into question public assurance, a rigorous self-scrutiny, more persistent than among the Elizabethans, supplied a strong motif to both poetry and prose, a marked component in the work of Milton, Donne and the Metaphysicals, Richard Baxter and William Laud, Robert Burton, John Bunyan, and Sir Thomas Browne.[8]

Of these, the last two left behind the best remembered formal "autobiographies." Often compared to the *Confessions*, which it resembles in piety and the evocation of guilt, though scarcely in intellectual sophistication, Bunyan's *Grace Abounding* describes a child's hellfire nightmares, a heavenly intervention in a game of tip-cat, a young man's colloquies with Satan—or his own perverse self-will—and after long darkness, a vision of redemptive love. All of this comes to us without much sensuous detail, but with a simple eloquence of speech, enriched by paraphrase and echo of the

English Bible, a kind of evangelical chapter-and-verse documentation; and from the first paragraph the didactic purpose of the personal history is explicit and unequivocal:

In this my relation of the merciful working of God upon my Soul, it will not be amiss, if, in the first place, I do, in a few words, give you a hint of my pedigree, and manner of bringing up; that thereby the goodness and bounty of God towards me may be the more advanced and magnified before the sons of men.[9]

Though it differs sharply in tone, Browne's *Religio Medici*, despite its breadth of learning, is no less limited in scope. Designed, as the preface indicates, not as a guide to conversion but as "a private Exercise directed to my self, . . . rather a memorial unto *me*, than an Example or Rule unto any other," it presents, with an odd mingling of quiet reason and quaint prejudice, a personal defense of Anglican faith and dogma, measured in the context of Christian theology, the Fathers of the early Church, including St. Augustine, and the Reformers since Luther. But, apart from preferences in the matter of belief and a few comments on moral attributes, it offers no particulars of personal experience. Browne the physician has surprisingly little to say of the physical life, the pains of adolescence and early manhood (he was about thirty years old at the time of writing), his travels, or his relationships with any actual community of men and women. "For the World," he tells us, in a characteristic metaphor, "I count it not an Inn, but an Hospital, and a place not to live but to dye in. The world that I regard is my self; it is the Microcosm of my own frame that I cast mine eye on; for the other, I use it like my Globe, and turn it round sometimes for my recreation." Accordingly, to the devout doctor, living is simply a kind of mortal interruption, and death is "the cure of all diseases," the panacea "which, though nauseous to queasie stomachs, yet to prepared appetites is Nectar, and a pleasant potion of immortality."[10]

Had he been concerned with self-portraiture rather than religious self-appraisal, Browne might have found a conspicuous precedent in the *Essays* of Montaigne, familiar to English readers since 1603 in John Florio's translation. In the preface to the first volume Montaigne boldly defines his subject: "I desire therein to be delineated in mine own genuine, simple, and ordinary fashion, without contention, art, or study; for it is myself I portray. . . . Thus, gentle reader, myself am the groundwork of my book." No earlier writer had done so much to secularize Christian introspection. But the finished work is neither an autobiography in discontinuous parts nor a sequence of confessions. It is a distillation of the ideas and impressions that the author has gained from personal experience and reflection, always with the sense that his life has been more or less typical or, at any rate, essentially human in appetite, emotion, and response. Many of the essays treat of apparently remote themes—cannibals, ancient philosophers, foreign social customs, a Spanish humanist—and there the self-portrait emerges only by indirection, in the personal tone, attitude, or judgment such materials evoke. Not until the last piece, "Of Experience," do we have an extended and comprehensive description of Montaigne's appetites and predilections, though still no account of his adventures, development, or career. "I study myself," he explains, "more than any other subject. It is my supernatural metaphysic, it is my natural philosophy." But self-study must bring no foolish "self-conceit"; the logic of his method assures a larger, disinterested result: "This long attention I employ in considering myself enableth me also to judge indifferently of others." From self-scrutiny he has learned how to assess a general human nature, what to value most highly and what to reject, and finally how best "to live this life well." He can teach himself and his reader no greater truth, for, he concludes, "There is nothing so goodly, so fair, and so lawful as to play the man well and duly."[11]

Among painters self-portrayal was not new in Montaigne's time, and it was almost standard practice in the years that followed. Its rise has been associated with the distribution throughout sixteenth-century Europe of well-crafted Venetian mirrors, which encouraged various kinds of self-contemplation.[12] But Albrecht Dürer, for example, who learned much of his art in Venice, scarcely needed an improved mirror to teach him fascination with his own perceptive self. The motives of the Renaissance self-portrait are difficult to determine. Often the mirrored self was simply the most readily available artist's model. Portraiture in general was expected to reveal more of the sitter's social status than of his individual personality. Details of clothing were accordingly of particular significance, insofar as apparel oft proclaimed the man, or, at any rate, the man's rank and occupation.[13] Later, in Rembrandt's scores of self-portraits, we find a more subjective impulse, a deeper reading of character and emotion; but since many of these are costume-pictures, we quickly detect Rembrandt's delight in role-playing, in his imagining for himself another calling in another age.[14] Eighteenth-century English self-portraits are self-conscious in another way, defensive, sometimes ironic, often self-flattering. Gainsborough painted himself at several stages of his career, not so much to celebrate his profession as to record his personal growth. Sir Joshua Reynolds' self-portrait, made for the Florentine

Academy and done with great panache, his academic velvet tam like a tilted halo, incurred Blake's ill-humored satire:

> Sir Joshua sent his own Portrait to
> The birth Place of Michael Angelo,
> And in the hand of the simpering fool
> He put a dirty paper scroll,
> And on the paper, to be polite,
> Did "Sketches by Michael Angelo" write.
> The Florentines said, " 'Tis a Dutch English bore,
> Michael Angelo's Name writ on Rembrandt's door." . . .
>
> These Verses were written by a very Envious Man,
> Who, whatever likeness he may have to Michael Angelo,
> Never can have any to Sir Jehoshuan.[15]

(Nor does Blake's rather bare drawing of himself, left in the Rossetti manuscript, have much resemblance in intention or effect to Sir Joshua's.) The self-obsessed James Barry depicted himself many times as a neglected hero and in late life as a weary sad-eyed moralist. Hogarth painted himself, with self-mocking detail and appropriate wit, sketching a grotesque Comic Muse. And the irrepressible Angelica Kauffman, delicately self-assured, painted herself, brush in hand—painting herself, perhaps, for the tablet before her is turned away from us.[16]

Autobiography sets the self-portrait in time and motion, presenting, as it does, a changing personality, developing, declining, remembering, regretting, rather than a fixed and finite impression. If the painter, deliberately or not, may distort his own mirror-image, the autobiographer, drawing on a sometimes distant past, unsure of his real achievement, forced to interpret the undeclared intentions of others who have crossed his path, is more susceptible still to error and clouded vision. Dr. Johnson assumed that the author of a self-history knew the truth with a certainty which "not only excludes mistake but fortifies veracity" and that he could have no cause "for falsehood or partiality except self-love."[17] But knowledge of the self is at best less certain and complete than Johnson suspected, and self-love, though capable of many disguises, is but one source of distortion. Describing and attempting to label the new literary form, Isaac D'Israeli was less assured of the truth of "self-biography," for the man who writes of himself, he warned, runs the danger of deceiving or being deceived, or falling into "the extravagance of vanity, and the delirium of egotism." The good "self-biographer" must use a simple, natural style and "be careful not to overshade and adorn his sketch, by a penciling too elaborate." Accordingly, though impressed by Rousseau's effusing "his inflammable soul in burning periods," D'Israeli concludes that most "self-biographers" will be safer to emulate the "attic simplicity" of David Hume.[18]

Fearful that to talk of himself at any considerable length would indeed be an exercise in vanity, Hume resolved to keep the *Life . . . Written by Himself* very short. The result is an unrevealing record of the books he published and the reception they received, an account doubly disappointing insofar as it comes from the philosopher credited with helping to formulate the modern concept of the self. Though clearly enough written, the narrative is more interesting for its omissions than for the materials it includes. Having cited his birth and made a few brief comments on his family background, Hume immediately leaps over twenty-two years of boyhood and youth, as if his formative period could be of no lasting interest to himself and of no concern to his readers. He is eager to tell us of the sensible "plan of life" he adopted in early maturity: "I resolved to make a very rigid frugality supply my deficiency of fortune, to maintain unimpaired my independency."[19] The plan, he is glad to say, proved successful; in due course Hume managed to achieve a relative prosperity without much sacrifice of companionship or good cheer. But rigid economy is not the most appealing of human virtues, whatever its happy consequence. We have learned from other examples to ask more of the autobiography of a great man than an object lesson in frugality.

As we might expect, Edward Gibbon's *Memoirs of My Life and Writings*, published posthumously in the same year as D'Israeli's article, is an altogether ampler and less frugal reminiscence. Gibbon is aware of the tradition to which he is contributing, stronger on the Continent than in England; he is familiar with Montaigne, whose irony anticipates his own, and with St. Augustine and Rousseau, who "disclose the secrets of the human heart." At the outset he claims for his personal history a "naked unblushing truth," though his method, as he proceeds, entails a careful selection of true details upon which he may base Gibbonian generalizations about human experience. He remembers—rather impatiently—being a sickly little boy, miserable at public school, deprived by his mother's early death of much needed sympathy, and he is ready to protest against the myth of childhood bliss which he hears "echoed with so much affectation in the World": "That happiness I have never known; that time I have never regretted." To the growing pains of youth he distinctly prefers the satisfaction of a "vigorous maturity." His career at Oxford affords evidence of the indolence and emptiness of English universities and provides a sharp contrast to the Swiss education, under a tutor at Lausanne, which made him a citizen of Europe. His thwarted love for

Suzanne Curchod, who became the celebrated Mme. Necker, leads to a somewhat circumspect reflection on the joy of sex: "The discovery of a sixth sense, the first consciousness of manhood is a very interesting moment of our lives; but it less properly belongs to the memoirs of an individual than to the natural history of the species." He then offers a second, and no doubt the real, reason for excluding the amatory affairs that many other memoirists have been all too eager to exploit: "The pains and pleasures of the body how important soever to ourselves are an indelicate topic of conversation." Gibbon's politer discourse centers on the private studies for the public writings that made his reputation, and on the leisurely travels that lengthened his perspectives. His cool commonsensical reason, distrustful of all sentiment, determines his disconcerting attitude towards the death of his father: "Few, perhaps, are the children who, after the expiration of some months or years, would sincerely rejoyce in the resurrection of their parents; and it is a melancholy truth, that my father's death, not unhappy for himself, was the only event that could save me from an hopeless life of obscurity and indigence."[20] As his father's heir, with neither a need for Hume's frugality nor yet with any stupefying excessive wealth, he can now enjoy the comfortable independence he considers the right and necessary condition for the historian. He may live the life of the self-sufficient bachelor, frequenting the best clubs in London or retreating at will to his well-stocked library. And his *Memoirs* presumably may serve as a guide to all gentlemen-scholars of fortunate circumstances and talent.

Many years later Mark Pattison claimed he had profited by the example. In his own autobiography he commends Gibbon's apologia: "The minute history of a self-education, conducted on so superb a scale, was just what I wanted. . . .

Gibbon, in fact, supplied the place of a college tutor; he not only found me advice, but secretly inspired me with the enthusiasm to follow it." Omitting all of his childhood and "boyish years" from his life story, Pattison begins the narrative with his coming up to Oxford, which, like Gibbon, he treats with some acerbity:

> I am fairly entitled to say that, since the year 1851, I have lived wholly for study. There can be no vanity in making this confession, for, strange to say, in a university ostensibly endowed for the cultivation of science and letters, such a life is hardly regarded as a creditable one.

But Pattison's irony scarcely matched Gibbon's, and his memoir, centered narrowly on self-improvement and the effort to free the mind "from the bondage of unreason," must have seemed merely solemn, arid, and quite old-fashioned when it appeared in 1885.[21] Other Victorians, at any rate, looking back to the eighteenth century, though still respectful of the reasonable Gibbon, might have seen a clearer anticipation of modern autobiography in the passionate *Confessions* of Rousseau.

The fame or notoriety of Rousseau was well established in Britain long before the publication of his personal history. Boswell knew enough of him to curry his favor, and Johnson, enough to respond, "Rousseau, sir, is a very bad man." Horace Walpole regarded him as an imposter, and Edmund Burke attacked his monstrous vanity. Hume, on the other hand, suspecting something like genius, brought him to England, where he began his *Confessions* and shortly afterwards declared himself the victim of his benefactor. When he eventually assailed Hume in a long, excited, paranoidal letter, Hume replied with a relatively mild *Exposé succinct*, which served only to further the legend. Translated soon after its appearance in Geneva, Rousseau's autobiography confirmed and magnified both the negative and the positive judgments and passed along to the new Romantic generation the image of a remarkable, though self-deluded, cultural hero. Byron thought him an "illustrious . . . madman," but nonetheless strove to retrace his steps in Switzerland, and introduced him, not unsympathetically, into *Childe Harold* as "the self-torturing sophist, wild Rousseau, / The apostle of Affliction, . . . who threw / Enchantment over Passion." And Shelley in his last great poem, "The Triumph of Life," called upon him to explain how all mortals had been betrayed by earthly ambition or desire, and he, Rousseau, more than any other, by his own susceptible heart, "which neither age, / Nor tears, nor infamy, nor now the tomb / Could temper to its object."[22]

Though now probably Rousseau's best known work, the *Confessions* must still compete for attention with our general knowledge of the man and his influence as a social and literary force. It is difficult to disengage the book from prejudice or pre-understanding, to appraise it as an autonomous unit and as a decisive contribution to the developing genre. In the beginning Rousseau affirms his personal uniqueness and the complete originality of his project:

I have entered upon a performance which is without precedent, whose accomplishment will have no imitator. I intend to present my fellow-mortals with a man in the integrity of nature; and this man shall be myself.

I know my heart, and have studied men; I am not made like any one I have met, perhaps like no one in existence. If not better, I at least claim originality, and whether Nature did wisely in breaking the mould with which she formed me, can only be determined after having read these books.

At the end, having again and again insisted upon his absolute candor, he declares that any sincere student of his
character who pronounces him "a dishonest man" clearly
"deserves a gibbet." The honesty (even in the French sense
of natural probity or trustworthiness) is certainly question-
able, insofar as it does not preclude a great deal of rationalizing and self-deception, a failure to recognize the distortions
of an overweening egoism. But, if we can set aside our
expectation—in fact, repeatedly fulfilled—of encountering
the willful exhibitionism of an already familiar Jean-Jacques
Rousseau, we may agree that the apparent frankness of
sustained self-revelation, the effort to discover and present
not a type but a complex individual like no one else in all
the world, does indeed set a precedent for modern autobiography.

Part of the freshness of the *Confessions* lies in its new
emphasis on childhood and adolescence, the formative years
that Hume and Gibbon thought hardly worth discussing.
Though he cannot remember exactly when he learned to
read, Rousseau vividly recalls his emotional response to
rather wide reading at the age of five or six: "from that
moment I date an uninterrupted knowledge of myself."
Denying any trace of "natural vanity," he admits to other
childish faults, to being "talkative, a glutton, and sometimes
a liar," and to making "no scruple of stealing sweetmeats."
His mother having died at his birth, he suggests that his
father half-resented and half-idolized him. From his aunt
he obtained a much needed tenderness and, on being punished by her, a somewhat sinister satisfaction: "All this
affection, aided by my natural mildness, was scarcely sufficient to prevent my seeking, by fresh offences, a return
of the same chastisement; for a degree of sensuality had
mingled with the smart and shame, which left more desire

than fear of a repetition." The punishment, he believes, influenced his adult sexual attitudes, for he has ever since enjoyed being subdued by imperious women. A less pleasing episode, however, remains traumatically vivid fifty years later: the experience of injustice, a beating from his uncle for a misdemeanor he did not commit. The most grievous offense of his youth, his stealing a ribbon and ascribing the theft to an innocent chambermaid, remains to trouble his dreams with conflicting emotions, shame, delayed remorse, self-consciously exploited compunction, and self-pity (but no real compassion for the disgraced girl). Indeed the burden of guilt and the longing for relief has, he claims, "contributed greatly to the resolution of writing my Confessions."[23] The early years, recollected with more passion than tranquillity, have thus done much to determine both the course of the subsequent life and the shape of the life-history.

Whatever sort of absolution could follow (and none seems likely), "confession" for the ease of conscience is clearly a recurrent motive behind Rousseau's autobiography, and St. Augustine must have provided a remote example of the method. But the confessing now leads to no conversion and draws no other men away from the paths of sin. Rousseau in the act of writing is still troubled, frightened, suspicious, and vindictive. He has found no release from a fearful paranoia; he remains in self-analysis, the patient and the psychiatrist perplexed by his own case-record. Yet, if the probing yields endless data for him to interpret, the process of reflection upon his character and conduct reveals more evidence for our appraisal than he suspects. His tearfulness and transports of bliss at the sight of chaste femininity seem to us excessive even in the context of eighteenth-century sensibility. His unprovoked changes of course and his sudden shifts of mood suggest an instability he will not acknowledge. He sees the cruelty of abandoning his sick friend Le Maître stricken on the street in Lyons, but he is still half-willing to excuse the enormity of his action with specious reasoning, ready always, as Byron charged, to "cast / O'er erring deeds and thoughts, a heavenly hue / Of words."[24] The second part of his book, though it describes the great success of his writings, becomes increasingly a self-defensive catalogue of his misfortunes, a long complaint of suffering and imagined persecution, and so in unintended ways a testament of constant neurosis and occasional madness.

Nonetheless, the appeal of the *Confessions* reaches beyond a concern with the perverse psychology of genius. We look to Gibbon's autobiography for information, and we may approach Rousseau's for the same reason, but we go on reading the latter because we find ourselves caught up in a spirited narrative. The author of *La Nouvelle Héloise* reveals his craft as a maker of fiction, no less than his passionate misadventures. If he is the anguished sentimentalist, he is also the inventive novelist fascinated by one Jean-Jacques Rousseau, the protagonist he is devising as much as remembering. But he is also able to call other characters into being, Madame de Warens, for example, or Thérèse le Vasseur, and to capture a setting with as much sensuous animation as necessary. He is aware of the picaresque tradition as he sets his hero out upon the road. Sometimes, speaking as that hero, he sounds a bit like Richardson's Pamela coyly describing a virtuous eroticism; sometimes, as the aggressive young man from the provinces, he seems to anticipate Stendhal's Julien Sorel. Like a novelist he knows the importance of trivial or casual detail, as when, leaping behind a lady on horseback and clasping her waist tightly, he comments, "Some women that may read this would be for giving me a box on the ear, and, truly, I deserved it."[25] And he knows, too, how to time each episode, for the leisurely pace of his manuscript allows him to give his memories at any moment appropriate fictional extension. Ultimately, of course, we judge the *Confessions* as a personal history and not as a novel; yet we cannot ignore in it the frequent approximation of the two genres. With Rousseau, autobiography for the first time draws freely on the resources of imaginative literature and, in so doing, begins to realize its full potential as a new literary form.

⋙ III ⋘

ELEMENTS OF AUTOBIOGRAPHY

> Anyway autobiography is easy like it or not au-
> tobiography is easy for any one and so this is to
> be everybody's autobiography.
>
> —*Gertrude Stein*

T HOUGH a herald of the whole European Romantic movement, Rousseau could have had no notion of the extremes to which Romantic subjectivity would be carried. But when he declared his *Confessions* without precedent and beyond imitation, he spoke accurately enough of French literature in his own time and of the French Romantic generation that followed. The memoir, centering on public affairs, intrigues, and personalities, was of course a well-established literary type in France, but the true autobiography, concerned like Rousseau's with the character of the writer, remained a relatively alien genre. The most sedulous "imitators" of the form Rousseau developed spoke another language. Nearly a century after the *Confessions*, Larousse as the latest authority on French usage described "autobiography" as a term of *English* invention and as a practice still rare in France but conspicuously common across the Channel.[1]

In England Coleridge had responded with enthusiasm to the precedent that Wordsworth thought he had set in *The Prelude*. But he was already well disposed towards autobiography before he knew any such term, and at least ten years before he heard Wordsworth's memorable reading of the poem. "I could inform the dullest author," he told his friend Thomas Poole in 1797, "how he might write an interesting book. Let him relate the events of his own life with honesty, not disguising the feelings that accompanied them."[2] In the late Victorian period Leslie Stephen ventured the same opinion: "Nobody," he said, "ever wrote a dull autobiography."[3] To the years between the two belong many subjective confessional works no doubt approaching if not achieving dullness, but also most of the incontestably great autobiographies of the English nineteenth century: *The Prelude* itself and *In Memoriam*, De Quincey's *Opium Eater*, Newman's *Apologia pro Vita sua*, Mill's strenuous mental history, Darwin's relaxed personal assessment—and not long after Stephen's pronouncement, Ruskin's *Praeterita* and Wilde's *De Profundis*. These and others of less note developed, clarified, and by example defined the form.

Autobiography, construed simply as writing about the self, is an act that may assume many shapes and guises, the diary, the letter, the journal, the formal self-history, the subjective poem, the short or long fiction. Carlyle was thinking of the act when he praised Goethe for solving the problem of autobiography—that is, for his discretion in selecting only such personal details as it was proper and pertinent to disclose.[4]

But autobiography is also a form, a literary genre with its own conventions and expectations.[5] The ideal autobiography presents a retrospect of some length on the writer's life and character, in which the actual events matter far less than the truth and depth of his experience. It describes a voyage of self-discovery, a life-journey confused by frequent misdirections and even crises of identity but reaching at last a sense of perspective and integration. It traces through the alert awakened memory a continuity from early childhood to maturity or even to old age. It registers a commitment to the unity and mystery of the self or soul, both alone and among other human beings. And as a work of literature it achieves a satisfying wholeness. Yet it is never complete since the writer's life is necessarily still in process.

So defined, autobiography is distinct in its inwardness from other closely related subjective forms, which indeed often impinge upon it. It is less random and fragmentary than the journal or diary, and less spontaneous, for it demands considered reflection upon experience and a detachment gained only by distance in time. It is more comprehensive and more purposefully organized than the letter, unless indeed the letter is extended, like Wilde's *De Profundis*, into an elaborate apologia.[6] If the memoir, as often advertised, seeks to tell the "inside story" of one's career and social involvement, the autobiography concentrates on the inner life, hidden from all others and accessible only in part even to the author. When groping for a fitting term, Isaac D'Israeli compared the new form to the new biography of his time. Formerly, he said, only the lives of statesmen and heroes seemed interesting to the biographer, but now that the life of the mind was taken seriously, the uneventful lives of thinkers, including men of letters, qualified for study. The "self-biographer," he hoped, would likewise explore his own mind and imagination.[7] Autobiography in the nineteenth century, much of it literary in origin and concern, did turn inward to a fascinated analysis of the self; and biography, becoming less speculative, perhaps rebuffed by the more persuasive probing of the rival genre, moved away from psychological interpretation towards the verifiable factualism of "scientific" history.

An autobiography resembles a dramatic monologue, in which the speaker reveals what he will—and often more than he intends—of the essentials of his character and the inmost workings of his mind. But in the monologue the writer (say, Browning), standing at some ironic distance from his subject, expects us to deduce the real, as opposed to the apparent, feelings of the speaker (the Duke, for example, in "My Last Duchess," or Andrea del Sarto) and to question his motives in declaring himself. In an autobiography the writer and speaker are one and the same, asking to be credited with true confession, neither one more aware than the other of the extent to which unwittingly he may be giving himself away. Autobiography in one sense is always true, since the author, whatever his intention or unconscious self-deception, presents—in the very tone and emphasis with which he talks of himself—some of the materials we need to assess his actual personality. Yet we know in reading that we have something less than the whole truth, for the autobiographer has had a life larger than his book, much of which he has chosen to exclude. In a monologue or a first-person novel the narrator properly has no existence outside the fiction. But in an autobiography the narrator plays only a few of the many roles he has adopted as a living man. If he was famous in his time (and most great autobiographers were), we have seen him in other roles, and we have other sources—other books, works of art, or acts of public polity—by which to judge his achievement. We do not forget Rousseau's place as prophet of revolution and romanticism, when we measure the degrees of voluntary and involuntary self-exposure in the *Confessions*. John Stuart Mill, whom we respect as the strenuous apostle of liberty and often the most selfless of men, seems, to at least one sensitive reader, to be exhibiting in his autobiography "a certain poverty of nature" and "a monotonous joyless-ness," and his account of his honest yet ineffective parlia-mentary career appears "too self-important, too minutely egotistic, for the dry and abstract style in which it is told."[8] Even if the autobiographer deliberately contrives a *persona*, we are not deceived as to his identity. Though Henry Adams, writing in the third person, devises a frustrated failing young man to act out his experience, we readily equate the pro-tagonist with the disillusioned but not unsuccessful histo-rian who bears his distinguished name. The tacit agreement between writer and reader of autobiography prescribes that the text bear the test of an outside reality and that it not require, as a monologue or novel may, the willing suspen-sion of disbelief to establish its truth.

Autobiography, then, is both calculated self-portraiture and unintentional self-betrayal. As readers we reject what we know to be willful distortion of fact. Yet we do not ask absolute accuracy of detail. We are prepared to accept lapses of memory and confusions of impression caused by distance from the event, for we expect the writer not to provide a literal *curriculum vitae* but rather to reveal the cast of his mind and the mould of his personality. But all revelation is at best approximate, insofar as language itself is to a degree opaque. Tennyson, confessing himself, complained,

> I sometimes hold it half a sin
>   To put in words the grief I feel;
>   For words, like Nature, half reveal
> And half conceal the Soul within.

In similar terms Carlyle regarded the verbal symbol as "con-cealment and yet revelation," a necessary clothing of the pure idea or naked emotion. And, speaking as Teufelsdröckh's editor, he wryly condemned his hero's metaphorical mode; we suspect, he said, "that these Autobiographical Documents are partly a mystification."⁹ Exploiting language or hiding behind it, the autobiographer at any moment may be more guarded and less direct in his self-revealing than we might wish.

A good deal of the concealment, omission, and suppression may be prompted by the writer's natural reticence or his desire to protect himself and others. A few autobiographers, to be sure, display a delight in the opportunity of apparently uninhibited self-exposure. James Hogg is pleased to exhibit himself as a clown among poets, fascinated by his own antics, audacity, and pretension: "I like to write about myself: in fact there are few things which I like better. . . . Often have I been laughed at for what an Edinburgh editor calls my good-natured egotism. . . . But I care not."¹⁰ And Henry Miller makes of his *Rosy Crucifixion* a long, unembarrassed, uncensored self-celebration. But a measure of modesty drives the more typical autobiographer to a self-consciousness in speaking at length of himself and an apology of sorts for obtruding so much personal matter upon a reading public. The fear of appearing egotistic struggles against the need for confession or self-justification.

Many writers accordingly, especially in the Victorian period, seek to resolve the conflict by proving their personal histories representative of specific religious or intellectual positions held by groups of their peers and so presumably of interest to the social historian. Others expect their self-scrutinies to reveal something of a general psychology. Sir Egerton Brydges, for instance, a minor poet of the early nineteenth century, attempts to excuse his tediously long self-pitying autobiography on the grounds that "the knowledge of human nature is valuable even when exhibited in the mental movements of obscure men"; and again, near the end of his second volume, in the hope—no doubt a vain one—of securing a rereading, he points to the general truths he has discovered as the lasting merit of his work: "I am willing to suppose that my Memorials may give more satisfaction on a second perusal than on the first; because they contain a great deal of generalization." Stephen Spender puts the case more succinctly when he considers the aesthetic extension of the personal record: "In literature the autobiographical is transformed. It is no longer the writer's experience: it becomes everyone's. He is no longer writing about himself: he is writing about life."[11] Nonetheless, however universal the implication may be, autobiography as such keeps the individual constantly before us, and our attention is focused upon his single distinct personality rather than upon a generalized type.

Beatrice Webb, in *My Apprenticeship*, may seem to be offering a conspicuous exception to such a rule of subjectivity, for her narrative keeps moving away from her own inner life to prolonged considerations of the social context in which she learned and practiced "the craft of a social investigator." The most intimate parts of her history are selections from her manuscript diary. But these she dismisses as "mere jottings of facts and impressions." She insists at the outset that she has "neither the desire nor the intention of writing an autobiography," and if the record nonetheless comes often close to such, the journal portions remain too unmediated to achieve an autobiographer's due perspective on a life and character. At all events, as a sociologist, Beatrice Webb declares her allegiance to a general welfare rather than to a merely personal concern. "To me," she affirms, " 'a million sick' have always seemed more worthy of self-sacrificing devotion than the 'child sick in a fever,' preferred by Mrs. Browning's *Aurora Leigh.*"[12] That bias sanctioned Mrs. Webb's vigorous career in social work. But it attenuates *My Apprenticeship* as spiritual autobiography, insofar as the form typically requires the premise of interest in significant selfhood and something, too, of a poet's regard for remembered individual detail.

Augustus Hare, the most assiduous and circumstantial of Victorian autobiographers, described his six-volume personal record as an effort to rescue something "like a connected story from the great shipwreck of time."[13] The discovery of connection is perhaps the primary object of formal autobiography. The author, surveying his years of growth, development, acquisition, and loss, seeks to establish a continuity of self, an assurance of at least some small elusive fixedness and unity amid the terrors of perpetual change. His primary resource, like that of St. Augustine, his great exemplar, is memory as the evoking and, more especially, the correlation of characteristic expressive experience.

The process of remembering may, of course, bring frequent frustration and defeat. Hazlitt was perplexed to think that we forget so many of "our strongest impressions."[14] Herbert Spencer, alarmed at the unreliability of his memories, which were contradicted repeatedly, he said, by factual evidence in journals and letters, strove to base his autobiography on incontrovertible documents.[15] Bertrand Russell supplements his reminiscences with letters from various stages of his long career, and A. L. Rowse refreshes his vivid memory of a Cornish education with reference to boyhood diaries and an old notebook. Henry Green, in telling his story, speculates on the process and content of recollection: how much of our early life, he wonders, do we actually recall, and how much have we been told so often by our elders that we think we really remember it?[16] And in an age of photography many self-historians must ask which images of their remote past emerge from the unaided mind and which from the pages of a family album.

Nonetheless, memory remains to most autobiographers the essential and efficacious faculty. Even Green, who admits to forgetting most of his affluent youth, is impressed by the fact that "what has been enjoyed so much so many years ago will lie in wait to crop up again at any time."[17] Fascinated by his own traumas, De Quincey denied the possibility of our ever really forgetting anything, for the impressions we think lost in the great reservoir of the unconscious may at any moment return, alarmingly or consolingly, to the surface.[18] In the twentieth century Herbert Read's autobiography offers the most eloquent homage to memory, especially to the recollection of earliest childhood: "A mind without memories means a body without sensibility; our memories make our whole imaginative life," or, more fancifully, "memory is a flower which only opens fully in the kingdom of Heaven, where the eye is eternally innocent."[19]

Like Wordsworth, Read values the first responses of the child, both in themselves and as the determinants of "the larger patterns and subtler atmospheres" of the adult life. On the whole, the liveliest chapters of autobiography from the Romantic period through to our own time deal with the experience of childhood, recalled in sharp sensuous detail. The child, as Bertrand Russell explained, is less "cased in Self" than the man he will become, and the memory of "one's instinctive past" has "a vividness that becomes impossible later."[20] Only autobiography can recover the "instinctive" impressions of the formative years; without such knowledge of the subject's childhood, biography typically, as one recent historian suggests, "gives the ego an unfair advantage over the id."[21] The autobiographer, in search of the beginnings of selfhood, reaches as far as possible back into his unselfconscious past. Compton Mackenzie dated his recollections from the age of two.[22] Few others have claimed so memorable an infancy, but many cherish the reawakened sense of movement through a lost world of brighter color and ampler proportion. If Rousseau called attention to the child's pains and pleasures, Wordsworth reverently examined the quality of the child's sensibility, and the Victorians, especially Ruskin, influenced possibly by the autobiographical fiction of Dickens, registered with a new intimacy the psychology of a child's first affections and misgivings.[23]

In the recovery of the past, the autobiographer typically recognizes the dependence of the child on places and persons, the physical setting, and the family circle. He recalls, often in precise detail, the early house and his room in it as places of security and supports for his once amorphous, diffident, inquiring child-self. And he remembers the parents who hovered like protective or menacing deities above him. Autobiography indeed frequently represents the writer's effort to come to terms belatedly with his father or mother, to understand, as only the adult can, the vitality of his parents' being and the meaning of the relationship out of which he was born. If the father or mother has been stiflingly coercive or possessive, the writer may describe the course of his liberation or else the lingering power of obedience from which respect or love or fear has allowed no ultimate escape. In whatever guise, parents and guardians loom large as an autobiographical convention; we cannot forget the purposeful patriarchs of the Adams clan, the gigantic, resolute Dr. Darwin, the demanding, humorless

James Mill, the pietistic Margaret Ruskin and her hardheaded husband. Augustus Hare reveres his well-meaning yet often mistaken godmother, who adopted him when his indifferent parents gave him up like a package of unwanted nonreturnable merchandise. Edmund Gosse sees in the conflict between father and son the struggle between an orthodox and a liberal generation. Samuel Butler finds revenge for childhood suffering and suppression in his complacent semifictional caricature of the hypocritical Pontifexes.[24] Frank O'Connor records his early antagonism to a drunken father and his admiration of a patient mother. And V. S. Pritchett with an unfailing good humor presents the amusing trials of life with an eccentric father.

Among the major writers confronting their parents from the vantage point of later years, John Stuart Mill surprisingly acknowledges the most direct debt to an antecedent work of autobiography. As a young man—he tells us—at the time of his mental crisis, when his father's bleak rationalism seemed of no avail to him, he came upon Marmontel's *Memoirs* and was reduced to tears he did not know he could produce by the account of a father's death and a son's assumption of responsibility as head of a large family. If we examine the source, it is not difficult to imagine Mill's effort at identification and his painful sense of difference. Marmontel's father, like Mill's, was prudent, severe, and often disagreeable. But it is not necessary to assume, as some psychologists have speculated, that Mill had secretly wished his father dead and now felt guilty of unfaithfulness; it may be enough to suggest that as the eldest child he was distressed to know that he felt no affection, comparable to the French youth's, for his mother and younger siblings. Marmontel with enviable overstatement recreates a scene worthy of the old sentimental drama, the *comédie larmoyante*.

On learning of his father's death, the sixteen-year old rushes home in the middle of the night and at once summons the whole grieving family:

I never felt so superior to myself. I had to raise an enormous weight of grief; I did not sink under it. . . . I received them all with the assurance of a man inspired by heaven, and without manifesting weakness, without shedding a tear, I, who weep so easily.

"Mother, brothers, sisters, we experience," said I to them, "the greatest of afflictions; let it not overcome us. Children, you lose a father, and you find one; I am he, I will be a father to you; I embrace all his duties; you are no longer orphans." At these words, rivers of tears, but tears much less bitter, flowed from their eyes.[25]

The young hero, then justly tired, stalks boldly off to sleep in his father's bed. Mill was capable of no such heroics, but the very fact that he clearly remembered the scene and its impact many years after his reading and at the time of writing his own history indicates his awareness of parallels in the autobiographical tradition.

Since the time of *The Prelude*, if not before, the education of the self has been a dominant theme in serious autobiography. The learning process is, of course, far larger and longer than the routine of school and its courses of pre-scribed study. Wordsworth learned much from nature, a good deal from books, and relatively little at Cambridge, where, he decided, an empty ritual prevailed and "imagination slept." Darwin, who thought his Cambridge years intellectually wasted, though socially a great pleasure, found his genuine educative experience aboard the *Beagle*. The education of Henry Adams reached far beyond his residence at Harvard College. And the erudition of Mill, gained at home, was more formidable than any he could have acquired at the newly founded Benthamite University of London. Nonetheless, school and college as specific places do play a considerable role in autobiography. The English writer—C. S. Lewis or Henry Green, for example—remembers with mixed emotions the public school, to which he was consigned as a lonely child abandoned "for his own good" by his well-intentioned parents. In *A Georgian Childhood* Cyril Connolly goes so far as to suggest that the great public schools are responsible for the "permanent adolescence" of the British ruling class, insofar as the experiences of the schoolboys, "their glories and disappointments, are so intense as to dominate their lives, and to arrest their development." The result, Connolly concludes, is that "the greater part of the ruling class remains adolescent, school-minded, self-conscious, cowardly sentimental, and in the last analysis, homosexual."[26]

The university in retrospect generally fares somewhat better. Newman writes with unusual warmth of the fellowship at Oriel, his first meeting with John Keble, and even his misguided "liberal" teachers. And C. S. Lewis remembers undergraduate Oxford as the setting of a special kind of "joy," the aesthetic experience of good talk for its own sake. Evelyn Waugh and Graham Greene, on the other hand, recall misspent Oxford years, academic indifference, ennui, and bouts of willful drunkenness; and Henry Green insists that his real life began only when he left the brittle culture of Oxford behind for the crude vitality of his father's Birmingham factory.[27] All in all, formal education brings little satisfaction to the autobiographer; and not much perhaps is to be expected, for autobiography typically recounts the struggle of the individual to find himself and his personal salvation beyond the confines of the current establishment.

To the self-historian development regularly involves severe crisis and eventual recovery of purpose. Graham Greene's response to school was a boredom deepening into suicidal depression, involving repeated experiments with "Russian roulette" and necessitating a prolonged psychiatric treatment. Mill's education gave him no desire to work for its rational objectives, and no answer to the urgent question of his troubled youth, was he "bound to go on living?" Kenneth Clark in a lively self-assured memoir reports a similar paralysis of the will, a profound melancholia, which overtook him at the age of sixteen, depriving him of "animal faith" and the conviction that anything was worth doing.[28] What Clark diagnoses as "accidie" and Mill calls "a crisis in my mental history," we may relate to the "identity crisis" defined by Erik Erikson, in which the young person loses for a time the coherence of selfhood, the "subjective sense of an invigorating sameness and continuity," and all confidence that the "style of one's individuality" has any real place in a larger social context.[29] The identity crisis recurs with variations in the personal writings of Wordsworth, Carlyle, Tennyson, Newman, Darwin, Ruskin, C. S. Lewis, Edwin Muir, and many others. Each of these records some need to transcend the despair that is the fear of death and the denial of life; each at length achieves a high measure of Erikson's "ego integrity" or "the ego's accrued assurance of its proclivity for order and meaning," each realizes his mature identity by finding his work and his role in society.[30] "Bringing order into my past experiences," writes Gerald Brennan in *A Life of One's Own*, "has . . . been the principal motive that I have had in writing this book."[31] The search for a pattern of order is the guiding impulse in nearly all autobiography, and the perception of some superintending design in the individual life determines the choice among remembered incidents and emotions and the weight attached to the selected episodes.

In the last analysis the autobiographer's review of his past is essentially an act of deliverance, a chronicle of resolved crisis and itself an affirmation of ordered meaning.[32] According to Stephen Spender, drawing on his own experience, "the basic truth of autobiography" is the individual's realization, "I am alone in the universe."[33] And the loneliness, as remembered by Mark Rutherford, may reach fearsome proportions, may become "the nameless dread, the efflux of all vitality, the ghostly haunting horror which is so nearly akin to madness."[34] Yet the confronting of the isolated self even retrospectively may prove therapeutic; the sense of alienation may engender the yearning for some religious communion or its secular counterpart. C. S. Lewis considered an ineluctable desire the driving force of his spiritual being, the *selige Sehnsucht* of Goethe:

> Und so lang' du das nicht hast,
> Dieses: Stirb und werde!
> Bist du nur ein trüber Gast
> Auf der dunklen Erde.[35]

The paradoxical dying into life, the finding of the self by losing the self, distinguishes true autobiography from the gossipy memoir and the anecdotal career history. The writer is concerned less with the the color of physical event than with something like the theological concept of *kenosis*, the emptying of the self, the pouring out of the self into a new or revitalized identity, or, in effect, simply the opening up of the consciousness to a new revelation. Though secularized by Joyce and popularly misunderstood ever since, the "epiphany," the Wordsworthian "spot of time," the moment of insight that transforms the soul or, less dramatically, alters the mental perspective, recurs with a good deal of its original religious significance throughout serious autobiography. Even so determined a skeptic as Bertrand Russell describes the shattering impact of a genuine epiphany: in this instance, an upwelling of sympathy with all human pain as he witnessed the paroxysms of a friend, Mrs. Alfred North Whitehead, suffering a severe heart attack, and at once leapt to conclusions of an oddly naive profundity:

She seemed cut off from everyone and everything by walls of agony, and the sense of solitude of each human soul suddenly overwhelmed me. . . . Within five minutes I went through some such reflections as the following: the loneliness of the human soul is unendurable; nothing can penetrate it except the highest intensity of the sort of love that religious teachers have preached; whatever does not spring from this motive is harmful, or at best useless; it follows that war is wrong, that a public school education is abominable, that the use of force is to be deprecated, and that in human relations one should penetrate to the core of loneliness in each person and speak to that. . . .

At the end of those five minutes, I had become a completely different person.[36]

The major spiritual autobiographies in English are, like Russell's, records of becoming different persons, narratives of conversion, of recovering a lost identity, or discovering a new and meaningful self. Each develops its individual pattern and reaches its own particular resolution. Yet all invoke with intensity the principal conventions of the autobiographical genre.

~§ IV ⮞~

AFTER *THE PRELUDE:* Spiritual Autobiography from Wordsworth to Muir

> There are in our existence spots of time,
> That with distinct pre-eminence retain
> A renovating virtue, whence, depressed
> By false opinion and contentious thought,
> Or aught of heavier or more deadly weight,
> In trivial occupations, and the round
> Of ordinary intercourse, our minds
> Are nourished and invisibly repaired.
>
> —*Wordsworth*

WITH his own notions of poetic style, Longfellow found *The Prelude* of 1850 disconcertingly uneven, the "lofty passages" punctuated by sudden lapses into the blankest prose. "It soars and sinks," he complained, "and is by turns sublime and commonplace."[1] With our less restricted view of an appropriate language for poetry, we may still be distressed by Wordsworth's frequent prosiness, as in the passage at the end of the often magnificent Book I, which painstakingly and anticlimactically informs Coleridge, the "honoured Friend," that autobiography has provided a safer and easier subject matter than a strenuous creativity would demand:

> One end at least hath been attained; my mind
> Hath been revived, and if this genial mood

Desert me not, forthwith shall be brought down
Through later years the story of my life.
The road lies plain before me;—'tis a theme
Single and of determined bounds; and hence
I choose it rather at this time, than work
Of ampler or more varied argument,
Where I might be discomfited and lost:
And certain hopes are with me, that to thee
This labour will be welcome, honoured Friend![2]

One of the earliest reviewers, on the other hand, regretted
that *The Prelude* had not been written, like most autobiographies, entirely in prose, which would readily have admitted the anecdotes and gossip of a memoirist.[3] Wordsworth,
however, more intent on registering sublimity than on providing amusement, required a medium flexible enough not
only to record the essential facts of his development but
also to accommodate the grandeurs of his experience. The
prosiness in effect helped him to authenticate the poetic
vision and to establish its credibility in a world of ordinary
things. Describing an unforgettable "spot of time," he writes:

It was, in truth,
An ordinary sight; but I should need
Colours and words that are unknown to man,
To paint the visionary dreariness
Which, while I looked all round for my lost guide,
Invested moorland waste and naked pool. . . . [4]

Repeatedly, with a too literal yet quite characteristic insis-
tency, he reminds us of the "ordinary" out of which the
extraordinary perception arises. His purpose is not to produce a chatty prose memoir but to recognize the matter-of-
factness of secular autobiography, to transcend it at will,

and ultimately to give the genre a new and decisive spiritual dimension.

Unevenness of style was apparently of small concern to Wordsworth, for it persists in all versions of *The Prelude*. Nevertheless, no major autobiography was ever more carefully reshaped and revised over so long a period. The more or less finished two-part poem of 1799 became a work in progress of epical proportions, the greatly extended *Prelude* of 1805 in thirteen books, which was still subject to innumerable changes, subtractions and additions, at least until 1839. Wordsworth was thoroughly aware of his purpose and his aesthetic means. Though he reworked his narrative throughout a long maturity, he kept it within fixed time limits as a Bildungsroman centered wholly on childhood, adolescence, and initiation, a portrait of the artist as a young man. Repeatedly within the text he speaks of the "song" he is composing.[5] He moves deliberately from a record of disappointment and despair to a more positive, "comedic" resolution: "Not with these began / Our song, and not with these our song must end." But the ending is delayed, and he self-consciously alludes to the unusual length of his poem as a whole, "this Song, which like a lark / I have protracted, in the unwearied heavens / Singing." Early in the argument he remarks that his "Song might dwell / On that delightful time of growing youth" when the spell of language for its own sake, the magic ring of phrases, first struck him with peculiar pleasure. Some of his deepest intimations, he confesses, lie "far hidden from the reach of words," never to be adequately translated into signs or symbols, and all literature often falls short of its aspiration. Yet books have had a real and lasting influence on his imagination, and even the tellers of fabulous tales are to be commended for their transcending of time and space, to make "our wish our power, our thought a deed." Despite Matthew Arnold's complaint that Wordsworth might profitably have read more widely, *The Prelude* bears constant witness to a sensibility thoroughly dedicated to the literary medium, steeped in a literary tradition, and prepared at times even to confuse the actual and the imagined and so to lend remembered experience a "texture midway between life and books."[6]

In Wordsworth's psychology the primary sensation of sight and sound, the actual evidence of "life," is, of course, essential, but it matters little until it has been assimilated and interpreted by the poetic imagination or, as we might say, made to some degree literary and even "bookish." The noisy whirl of London, presented vividly enough in Book VII, makes no deep impression on the poet, and even the theater, in which he takes some real delight, has but a transitory power, for the emotions it evokes—as he declares in a metaphor appropriate to the context—pass "not beyond the suburbs of the mind." He fears that sometimes in the pursuit of pleasure he may have betrayed the inner vision. As an undergraduate he was, he says, all too content with light-hearted companions, "unthinking natures, easy minds / And pillowy," and he considers the frivolities of his college years to represent "an inner falling off" from the yearnings of his earlier youth. Later he tells us how he has had to resist the tyranny of "the bodily eye," which, as "the most despotic of the senses," has "often held [his] mind / In absolute dominion." His orientation is not complete until he can establish the supremacy of "the intellectual eye," the imaginative insight, as master of the inner city of his being. The theme of his autobiography as a whole, he announces at the end, has been Imagination and Intellectual Love. These are the ideals by which he must measure his growth as poet from the moment when, home from Cambridge, walking through the night into a summer sunrise, he had his first awareness of distinct vocation:

> My heart was full; I made no vows, but vows
> Were then made for me; bond unknown to me
> Was given, that I should be, else sinning greatly,
> A dedicated Spirit.[7]

Though he seems, when most prosaic, excessively literal in his insistence on the precise impression, Wordsworth moves inevitably as the dedicated Spirit from the analytic method, which examines all facts for their evidential value, to the mode of synthesis, which demands only such data as are relevant to a coherent pattern. However profoundly he is committed to a faith in the power of memory, he is nonetheless able to forget or suppress inconvenient detail. His autobiography has accordingly been attacked for its omissions and distortions, its failure, for example, to mention the relationship with Annette Vallon, except, perhaps, obliquely in the tedious story of Vaudracour and Julia, or to admit any personal limitations beyond those inner fallings-off, the lapses into superficial thought and feeling. But *The Prelude* is never really a "confession," in the primary sense of that word as an acknowledgment of guilt. Augustine, confessing, asks forgiveness for sins of body and mind, and Rousseau, with a too proud contrition, exposes meanness and perfidy, but Wordsworth owns to nothing really culpable or shameful. His poem by design is less confession than profession, a testimony of integrating insight and finally well-earned equipoise.

The Prelude moves back and forth from general commentary and summary narrative to set description of incidents evoked in sharp visual detail. The growth of the poet's mind is an education by epiphany, by "spots of time"—or, more accurately, of timelessness—when the interval expands qualitatively and the instant becomes the eternal now. Not all the memorable moments, of course, are so privileged or to be recalled with great reverence. The calculated gesture at the fallen Bastille, for example, yields no positive result; the poet remembers pocketing a stone, "in the guise / Of an enthusiast," and all the while "Affecting more emotion than [he] felt."[8] By way of contrast, the meeting of a haggard French peasant girl, languidly leading a heifer, makes a decisive impression, converting him at once to the Revolutionary cause and to his friend Beaupuy's conviction, " 'Tis against *that* / That we are fighting."[9] Yet even this incident is more purposive, more open to rational explanation, than the genuine "spot of time," which must stand as an illumination in itself rather than as a means to some ideological end.

The not-dissimilar sight of the Cumberland girl with a pitcher on her head, making her way painfully against a strong wind, has a quite different, a less logical implication; it remains as the aesthetic arrangement of indescribable suggestion, an image of "visionary dreariness" in itself and of no immediate political or social consequence. Here the impact of a true epiphany depends on a prior state of bewilderment and loss of direction, and entails the receiver's transcendence of self-consciousness as if he were emptied of self altogether and readied for a larger revelation. Remembering the experience in after years, the poet declares, "I am lost"—that is, detached once again from the imperious demand of the present—and in the mood of abstraction he recovers something of the original strength and wonder of the stunned lost schoolboy's emotion.[10]

A like disorientation precedes his view of the blind beggar

in London; once again he is "lost," wandering bemused in a surging crowd, where he questions his own identity and where every passerby is yet another mystery, when "abruptly" he is "smitten" by the sight of the mendicant with a label pinned to his coat telling his name and plight:

> Caught by the spectacle my mind turned round
> As with the might of waters; an apt type
> This label seemed of the utmost we can know,
> Both of ourselves and of the universe;
> And, on the shape of that unmoving man,
> His steadfast face and sightless eyes, I gazed,
> As if admonished from another world.[11]

Most memorably, the sense of being "lost," bewildered, rapt away from mundane concerns, accompanies the greatest of Wordsworth's epiphanies, his apocalyptic vision at the Simplon Pass, which follows his disappointment at missing the high divide of the Alps:

> I was lost;
> Halted without an effort to break through;
> But to my conscious soul I now can say—
> "I recognise thy glory:" in such strength
> Of usurpation, when the light of sense
> Goes out, but with a flash that has revealed
> The invisible world, doth greatness make abode,
> There harbours whether we be young or old.
> Our destiny, our being's heart and home,
> Is with infinitude, and only there;
> With hope it is, hope that can never die,
> Effort, and expectation, and desire,
> And something evermore about to be.

The self lost at the Simplon Pass becomes the self restored, or to use the poet's word, "renovated," convinced anew of its essential continuity and value. The light of sense yields to the inner vision, the flash of "glory," which, according to the Intimations Ode, the child perpetually assumed. Ultimately, as the last book of *The Prelude* tells us, it is the role of the adult imagination, "that glorious faculty," to discover its true analogue in nature, as in the moon at Mount Snowdon brooding over dark abysses, "the emblem of a mind / That feeds upon infinity."

Not all autobiographers achieve, or even reach for, such sublime assurance. But many, probing the psychology of selfhood, record "spots of time" of peculiar significance, moments of heightened perception, and sometimes intimations of a dimension to human life ineluctably greater than the sum of its parts. Wordsworth's poem remains exemplary in its demonstration that the edge of meaning lies never far beyond the prose of ordinary experience.

De Quincey, though his formal medium is not poetry, shows much less regard for the prosaic fact. His *Autobiographical Sketches* and *Confessions of an English Opium-Eater* transport us to a quite unwordsworthian climate of perception, an unfamiliar exotic world of strange shapes and surrealistic magnitudes. Yet he acknowledges a distinct debt to Wordsworth, both as the "great modern poet," whose genius he declares himself the first to have recognized, and also as the Lake Country neighbor, with whom he has spent long hours in earnest conversation.[12] Reviewing his own troubled childhood, he digresses on the wisdom of Wordsworth's apothegm that "The Child is father of the Man," and he seems mindful of the poet's wish for "days . . . Bound each to each by natural piety," when he writes of the strength he has gained from his sense of "years that were far asunder . . . bound together by subtle links of suffering derived from a common root."[13] The most indelible of his own "spots of time" recalls the harmony of the Simplon Pass, where wind, rock, and sky, "the darkness and the light," merged as "types and symbols of Eternity / Of first and last, and midst, and without end." De Quincey describes the depths of a blue sky which "seemed the express types of infinity" and a wind that was "the one great audible symbol of eternity."[14] But the circumstances of De Quincey's epiphany, repeated, we are told, three times in his life, are more particular and idiosyncratic, less "ordinary," that those prompted by even the most exalted response to Alpine scenery, for they involve a death-chamber and a child, or child-like man, standing entranced at noon on a summer day between a corpse and a window open to the hot sunshine and the hollow-sounding wind.[15]

So described in a sketch from the 1830s, the situation seems contrived and scarcely credible, or, at any rate, too singular for its alleged recurrence. But De Quincey's literal accuracy was disputed as early as the first version of the *Confessions*, and "objectivity" *per se* was never his primary concern.[16] He suspected indeed that he might at times be mistaking his morbid fancies for *objective* entities—he italicized the word in 1821 and later glossed it as "apparently pedantic" yet all the same "indispensable" to one recognizing other levels of reality.[17] Seldom has autobiography been so subjectively oriented, so centered on a mind contemplating its own inventions. His "confessions" bear no resemblance to Rousseau's. Despite his lurid title, which might evoke dens of iniquity, he has no shameful private life, real or imaginary, to reveal, and no taste, in any case, for such exposure. He defends, almost to the point of ironic overstatement, the "delicate and honourable reserve" of his countrymen: "Nothing . . . is more revolting to English

feelings, than the spectacle of a human being obtruding on
our notice his moral ulcers or scars, and tearing away that
'decent drapery,' which time, or indulgence to human frailty,
may have drawn over them: accordingly, the greater part
of *our* confessions (that is, spontaneous and extra-judicial
confessions) proceed from demireps, adventurers, or swin-
dlers: and for any such acts of gratuitous self-humiliation
from those who can be supposed in sympathy with the
decent and self-respecting part of society, we must look to
French literature . . ."—presumably, first of all, to Rousseau.[18]

De Quincey's decent British confessions conceal as much
as they reveal; as soon as they approach areas of danger,
they begin to wander evasively in other directions. His style
is marked by constant digression, periphrasis, parenthesis,
long trains of free association which serve to distract attention from the matter in hand and remove the necessity of
direct commitment. If he feels any guilt, it is for what he
has been and is, not for anything he confesses to have done.
He is the innocent but also the pariah, at odds with the
society he claims to respect, in sympathy with other out-
casts, such as Ann the prostitute, the fallen angel of mercy,
and fascinated by antisocial conduct, murder, and all rebellious criminality. The pains of opium bring him visions
of torment and torture, sadism and masochism, a capacity
for which he is loath to admit in himself or in others. But
the deepest horror of his nightmares is that they involve
the dazed bystander, against all will and reason, in violent
action which they delude him into accepting, at least for
the time of possession, as real "objective" fact.

Whatever the garish derangements of its prolonged excessive use, opium, even as mild habitual sedative, confirmed and, as it were, sanctioned De Quincey's natural

passivity, his instinctive recessiveness, and what he himself called his "intellectual torpor."[19] And it encouraged a sort of subjective idealism, or idealizing, by which he reconstituted the outside world for his own convenience or contemplation. In the infinite reaches of the *Confessions*, all things perpetually recur and interconnect; space swells endlessly, and time expands to eons of consciousness, "far beyond the limits of any human experience."[20] The digressive mode is appropriate since in life there is no possible completion; one sensation or idea leads on inevitably to the next, and all impressions are ultimately one to the reminiscential mind. A Piranesi etching of broken flights of stairs, one above the other till all disappear into the gloom of a remote ceiling, and a lonely figure, toiling forever upwards, provides the image of a terrifying continuum.[21] The wanderer, alone in London crowds, knows a similar bewilderment, a reduction in the presence of vastness, where the streets branch off interminably or lose themselves in long diminishing perspectives. Time may accelerate or seem to linger; moments of insight qualitatively outweigh months of routine, but the respite is brief, and time itself relentless. Among the arts, music provides De Quincey the best chance of escape; a rich harmony of spreading sound places his whole life before him, purified, rationalized, released from temporal progression and the demands of engagement.

In the last part of the *Confessions* De Quincey, self-conscious always, even in his passivity and garrulous evasiveness, addresses the reader: "You will think, perhaps, that I am too confidential and communicative of my own private history. It may be so. But my way of writing is rather to think aloud, and follow my own humours, than much to inquire who is listening to me; for, if once I stop to consider what is proper to be said, I shall soon come to doubt whether any part at all is proper."[22] But his private history requires no apology for impropriety of conduct; it is less a chronicle of impetuous events than a sequence of moods and images, a meandering interior monologue in long-drawn periods, heightened by an erudite allusive style. It is an autobiography that spills over into other subjective sketches and essays, notably "The English Mail Coach" and "Suspiria de Profundis," continually creating and elaborating a self,[23] but in final effect projecting a temperament rather than a man, a sensibility disposed, as De Quincey himself tells us, "to meditate too much and to observe too little." The casement of his sister's death-chamber admits no earthly vision but a dazzling light. Another window, presented in the *Confessions*, looks into the dark to the sea below and a dim distant city. Before it, "more than once" (as we are assured and indeed might expect), sits the silent brooding opium-eater all night long, "from sun-set to sun-rise, motionless, and without wishing to move."[24]

Unlike De Quincey, Charles Darwin had some misgivings about his capacity for meditation but none at all about his powers as an observer. Rather, like David Copperfield, who, near the beginning of his life story, claims to have been "a child of close observation" and to be a man of strong circumstantial memory, Darwin throughout his *Autobiography* affirms his reverent regard for minute detail: "I think that I am superior to the common run of men in noticing things which easily escape attention, and in observing them carefully."[25] His method as a naturalist, he insists, is thoroughly inductive: from the beginning of the long researches that led to *The Origin of Species* "I worked on true Baconian principles, and without any theory collected facts on a wholesale scale." He finds Herbert Spencer's "deductive manner of treating every subject . . . wholly opposed to my own frame of mind." And he is disappointed by a second reading of his grandfather's *Zoönomia*, "the proportion of speculation being so large to the facts given." He himself has amassed mountains of fact to support his theories and has always, he testifies, tried to keep his mind open "so as to give up any hypothesis . . . as soon as facts are shown to be opposed to it."[26]

Nevertheless, he acknowledges a lifelong will to speculate on the evidence he has gathered, a need to maintain a perspective on his work and a continuity of experience. He questions the value of "inward convictions and feelings" as a reliable guide to faith, and he is discomfited to the point of illness by serious introspection or prolonged "meditation." But he is all the same consistently the "natural philosopher" (in the original sense of that term), eager to discern in nature the operation of some great law of being. The last sentence of *The Origin of Species* asserts a "grandeur in *this view of life*," and one of his personal letters suggests that some theory must guide experiment, or at least develop in the process of research, since "all observation must be for or against *some view* if it is to be of any service."[27] The *Autobiography* firmly establishes his philosophic bias, the deep-seated desire for synthesis. In his characterization of fellow-scientists he indicates not only his standard of judgment but also, when most positive, his ideal self-image. Thus John Henslow is a good and learned man, truly observant and disposed "to draw conclusions from long-continued minute observations," but no one "would say that he possessed much original genius"; Robert Murchison, though a celebrated geologist, is "very far from possessing a philosophical mind"; and Robert Brown, an immensely well informed botanist, seems incapable of propounding "any large scientific views." J. D. Hooker, on the other hand, "is very acute, and he has great powers of generalisation"; and Charles Lyell has shown enough patience and originality to develop and cogently defend the great general theory of uniformitarian change.[28] Darwin conceives of himself as both the close observer of distinguishing detail and the philosophical generalist seeking and finding a broad overview of all creation. He remembers having achieved, as early as the expedition of the *Beagle,* the power of concentrating his whole past knowledge on each new impression: "Everything about which I thought or read was made to bear directly on what I had seen and was likely to see; and this habit of mind was continued during the five years of the voyage."[29] So formed and nourished, this mental disposition, he is convinced, has persisted to the end and has done most to determine his ultimate success as natural philosopher.

Darwin's *Autobiography* recognizes the voyage of the *Beagle* as "by far the most important event" in his life. After his return to England come prodigious labors of research, followed by agonies of composition, resulting in volumes of lucid and apparently effortless expository prose. His rapid review of the monographs entails his restrained but frank assessment of their value to the scientific community and his statement of satisfaction with his growing reputation. When he has mentioned all his books, "the milestones in my life," he concludes that "little remains to be said."[30] Though he is addressing his children, he refers in only the briefest and vaguest terms to his perfect wife ("so infinitely my superior in every single moral quality") and his altogether exemplary sons and daughters, not one of whom has ever given him "one minute's anxiety, except on the score of health."[31] He gives the birth-date (but not the name) of his eldest son only because he wishes to explain that he was interested at the time in the systematic analysis of "expression" in men and animals, and the baby provided a ready subject for study. Though in life a devoted husband and father, he presents himself as more and more narrowly the scientist, gradually excluding aesthetic concerns but scarcely changing his cast of mind in any other way once he has found his career.

The first half of the narrative, however, describing Darwin's adolescence and apprenticeship, offers another image, less purposeful, but more animated and more engaging. The three years at Cambridge are presented as an almost complete waste of time academically but still "the most joyful in my happy life; for I was then in excellent health, and almost always in high spirits."[32] The joy arose in part from an intellectual awakening, largely extracurricular, remembered in vivid detail, the botanic walks and talks with men of science during term and on vacation, and the delights and hazards of collecting beetles (especially the occasion of his popping one rare specimen into his mouth to free his hand to seize another). The high spirits led to hunting parties and some mild roistering with "a sporting set, including some dissipated low-minded young men," but since the misspent days were jolly and the companions agreeable, the autobiographer "cannot help looking back to these times with much pleasure."[33] Eventually the collecting of beetles for beetles' sake subserves more disciplined scientific objectives, and the young barbarian zealous only for partridge-shooting yields to the civilized bird-watcher intent on detecting avian variations. But the gain involves loss; the vigorous sociable youth sinks into a neurotically recessive middle age, and the joy of unexpected event becomes the commonsense of organized routine.

The latter part of the *Autobiography* undoubtedly paints too bleak a picture, for the aging scientist who tells his story clearly retains—or is able to recover without noticeable strain—some of the emotion he believes atrophied. Nor has his aesthetic sense wholly disappeared, for it remains not only in an appetite for romantic novels but also, and more importantly, in the simple grace with which he reviews his past. To his great regret his sensibility has surely diminished with the years, but it was once too strong and various for its influence ever wholly to vanish. The early chapters describe his warm response to both poetry and music, an interest sufficient to make *Paradise Lost* his favorite reading on the *Beagle* or to induce him as an under-graduate to hire the choir boys from King's College Chapel to sing in his rooms at Trinity. Though he claims to have read *The Excursion* twice through from beginning to end, he apparently did not know *The Prelude;* but he scarcely needed Wordsworth's example to record his own "spots of time" with a poetic precision. He recalls his "thrill of delight" at S. Iago in the Cape Verde Islands when he suddenly determined to write a book on geology: "That was a memorable hour to me, and how distinctly I can call to mind the low cliff of lava beneath which I rested, with the sun glaring hot, a few strange desert plants growing near, and with living corals in the tidal pools at my feet." A letter from his sister reporting some scientists' praise of his fossil collection excites a more dramatic expression: "I clambered over the mountains of Ascension with a bounding step and made the volcanic rocks resound under my geological hammer." And the memory of a sudden intuition concerning the divergence of species has the distinct quality of a literary epiphany: "I can remember the very spot in the road, whilst in my carriage, when to my joy the solution occurred to me."[34]

The tone of such passages suggests not a derivation from Wordsworth and the Romantics but rather a degree of sympathetic alignment. The appeal in each instance relates an intensely subjective experience to a unified setting, a particular time and place. And a similar aesthetic sensibility, recurring throughout Darwin's scientific writings, animates the objective data of *The Origin of Species* with a special glow of conviction, a bemused irony, and an unceasing wonder.

If De Quincey's meditation leads to a subjective reverie ultimately indifferent to actual fact, Darwin's observation grounds his boldest theorizing in the world of "ordinary" experience, to which Wordsworth habitually made his appeal. An empirical bias not unlike that which was essential to the amassing of Darwin's evidence informs the spiritual and intellectual histories of many Victorians who had no comparable scientific eminence. Indeed it is the recurrent concern for real objective things that protects most of the major nineteenth-century autobiographers, subtle as they may be in self-analysis, from recourse to a wholly private subjectivity. Of all these, Ruskin is both the most probing in personal psychology and the most vivid in circumstantial sensuous detail.

Like Darwin, and with equal justification, Ruskin in *Praeterita* claims for himself the capacity of the acute observer. "I have never known one," he declares, "whose thirst for visible fact was at once so eager and so methodic." His "patience in looking and precision in feeling" have helped shape the "analytic power" he considers his greatest asset. His observations might well have taken a scientific turn; given the opportunity, he could, he insists, have become "probably the first geologist of my time in Europe." As it is, he has remained the collector of specimens. He remembers his ascent of Mount Snowdon not as the source of a Wordsworthian revelation but as the occasion of his delighted discovery of "a piece of copper pyrites." His attitude toward science, however, is hardly Darwin's or Lyell's. He impatiently dismisses Louis Agassiz' monograph naming fossil fishes, since "it didn't matter a stale herring to any mortal whether they had any names or not" (yet he commends the lithographer for supplying Agassiz with admirable illustrations).[35] He believes that any natural object seen intensely gives some clue to the created universe, but he regards the microscope as a base distorter of human vision. The truth to nature he seeks is an aesthetic realism, a respect for intricate line and color, as in his own close drawings of stratified rocks or curling tendrils.

Ruskin's preference of things actually seen to formal idealizations becomes at times excessive and eccentric, as when in Rome he repudiates the heroics of Raphael and Titian as less true than his own defiant effort to make "a careful study of old clothes hanging out of old windows in the Jews' quarter." By the same token he values Byron as the poet concerned with "real people" and the "truth of observation": "Of all things within the range of human thought [Byron] felt the facts, and discerned the natures with accurate justice." As a child Ruskin traveled, he tells us, with mother and father, not "for adventures, nor for company, but to see with our eyes, and to measure with our hearts." And throughout his adult life he has remained quite literally the "seer": "If you have sympathy, the aspect of humanity is more true to the depths of it than its words; and even in my own land, the things in which I have been least deceived are those which I have learned as their Spectator."[36]

Darwin's observation pours into his research; Ruskin's, into his art, his drawings, his criticism, and the animated supple prose of the autobiography that celebrates the gift of seeing. *Praeterita* not only announces its author's "skill of language": it abundantly illustrates it in terms of passion, wit, and irony, verbal play and facility, novelistic precision and fullness of image. It calls persons and places into being with a Dickensian force and color, the exuberance of superlatives, yet a detachment which assures the illusion of objectivity. It achieves the force of fictional narrative in its account of the drowning of a handsome cousin as he set off for Australia, or the meeting with the gentlemanly young Charles Eliot Norton on a steamer near Geneva, or the fate of a Swiss artist-friend, who, selling short his real talent, "went back to Berne and . . . made his black bread by dull portrait-painting to the end of a lost life." Its descriptions supply the significant detail that helps create a setting—the scurry of ants in the garden walk at Herne Hill, the layers of paint around the wine-merchant's office bell, the grim graceless iron pillars in an evangelical London chapel. An incompetent private tutor is emphatically remembered, without physical attributes, as a sad sign of the times: "a more wretched, innocent, patient, insensible, unadmirable, uncomfortable, intolerable being never was produced in this area of England by the culture characteristic of her metropolis." The college censor, on the other hand, is physically evoked as "a Christ Church Gorgon or Erinnys, whose passing cast a shadow on the air as well as on the gravel." Oxford in general, though asking acceptance, receives a cool critical response: "What an aesthetic view I had of all my tutors and companions, how consistently they took to me the aspect of pictures, and how I from the first declined giving any attention to those which were not well painted enough."[37] Thus the spectator, like the novelist or the scientist, maintains the distance essential to give his observations and impressions an independent objective substance.

Detachment in *Praeterita* extends to the self and its antecedents. Ruskin establishes a clear ironic perspective on the age he lives in, on the roles he has played, and on his actual status as the son of an affluent aspiring tradesman. He readily detects the foolishness of his father's ambitions for him as a gentleman-commoner at Oxford and a potential Archbishop of Canterbury, the condescension of his mother toward neighbors and poor relations, and the snobbish uneasiness of both parents in the presence of the titled happy few. Despite his respect for his father's mercantile integrity, he has no positive illusions about the process of moneymaking; brief encounters with the sherry-buyers his father brings to Herne Hill engender only "an extremely low estimate of the commercial mind as such." Though he affirms his early reverence for Alpine scenery, he recognizes that such a response to mountains would hardly have been possible before the age of Rousseau and the Romantics. He is acutely aware of a broad cultural context, and he sees himself at various stages as if he were a remote third person. He is now a child in a forbidden garden leading "a very small, perky, conceited Cock-Robinson-Crusoe sort of life," and now an awkward ingenuous young man, "in social behaviour and mind a curious combination of Mr Traddles, Mr Toots, and Mr Winkle." He remembers a rare befuddlement after a vinous college-initiation supper, as if he were David Copperfield describing his first dissipation: "I walked across Peckwater to my own rooms, deliberating, as I went, whether there was any immediately practicable trigonometric method of determining whether I was walking straight towards the lamp over the door." For the whole time at Oxford, he tells us, "I was, in all sorts of ways at once, less than myself, and in all sorts of wrong places at once, out of my place," and, again, "I was simply a little floppy and soppy tadpole."[38]

Yet his capacity for disinterested self-appraisal should not mislead us; the apparent detachment conceals and controls depths of subjective emotion and concern. He repeatedly defines himself and his needs in negatives. He explains his lack of childhood friends: "I was not myself the sort of creature that a boy could care much for." He counts early restraints and lessons of strict obedience among the blessings of his youth, yet considers the great calamity of his education the fact that it left him "nothing to love," not even father and mother, for they inspired respect rather than affection. When his cousin drowns, he feels little grief, "but much awe and wonder, when all the best and kindest of us are struck down, what my own selfish life was to come to, or end in."[39] His self-analysis is painful and deliberate; for some years he keeps a skull on his mantelpiece to look at before he goes to sleep. His greatest happiness, he confesses, has always been impersonal, coming when he knows no one is thinking of him or judging his conduct, when he can avoid the attention of others, as in early childhood he occasionally managed to elude his mother's watchful eye. But he must also escape his own nagging self-scrutiny to secure the peace and satisfaction of his role as alert disinterested spectator.

So compelling is the force of negation in *Praeterita* that some recent readers have found Ruskin perilously close to "sabotage of the self," ready to destroy his own identity and prepared in the process to "deconstruct" the autobiographical genre.[40] Yet we must not ignore the counterbalancing positive assertions of pride in observation and mastery of medium, the unconcealed delight in a capacity for "drawing delicately with the pen-point" and the self-assured command of language and "accuracy of diction" well beyond the reach of nearly all contemporary men of letters. To-

wards the end of *Praeterita* Ruskin cites, without embarrassment or conceit, Norton's praise of the already published
first volume as "the retrospect of a wise man" presented in
wonderfully "sharp-cut outline" and "fulness of light and
colour." From the beginning he affirms his respect for objective fact, however personal may be his response or idiom;
if his writings often "seem inordinately impressional and
emotional," he has never, he insists, yielded to "any manner
of illusion or false imagination," never been guilty, he might
have said, of what he himself called "the pathetic fallacy."
Though scarcely in truth so free from illusion as he claims
to be, he does maintain, at least until his last few paragraphs,
a considerable clarity of vision and an awareness of his
original resolve as autobiographer to talk only of what it
gives him joy to remember. But he associates such enjoy-
ment with neither close friendships nor public acclaim. He
finds his highest satisfaction, indeed his true identity in his
work, his mission as teacher. "How I learned the things I
taught," he declares, "is the major, and properly, only question regarded in this history." More "modest" autobiographers, he concedes, concentrate chiefly on the amusing or
distinguished people they have met; he, on the other hand,
has chosen to notice only "those who have had distinct
power in the training or pruning of little me to any good."
Thus the trained, pruned *me*, as if observed from outside,
becomes an object of fascinated attention: "As I look deeper
into the mirror," he remarks, "I find myself a more curious
person than I had thought."[41] If his narrative seems to us
often disinterested and almost selfless, the narrator remains
a distinct entity, more self-conscious than self-destructive.

By the 1880s Ruskin was impatiently dismissing Wordsworth as an artist lacking in both humor and the sense of
tragedy. In the same decade, however, he was invoking in

Praeterita "spots of time" more Wordsworthian than he suspected, moments of qualitative intensity that confirmed his purposes or redirected his energies.[42] His first enraptured response to the Alps relates—in the poet's way—dedication to setting: "I went down that evening from the garden-terrace of Schaffhausen with my destiny fixed in all of it that was to be sacred and useful." And soon afterwards, when he had taken "the grandest pass into Italy," the sight— or vision—of the mountains behind the marble-bright cathedral of Milan parallels Wordsworth's great experience at Simplon insofar as it, too, provides symbols of eternity, tokens of "seemingly immutable good in this mutable world." Less ecstatically but no less distinctly he remembers as a student noticing a snatch of ivy on the Norwood road, stopping to sketch it in minute detail, and suddenly perceiving in the process the importance, never taught him by his drawing master, of rendering "what was really there." The memory of a similar moment at Fontainebleau carries deep connotation; tired, depressed, ill, resting by the roadside—"lost," as Wordsworth would have described the condition—he concentrates attention on an aspen tree outlined against the sky and strives to recreate its configuration in his sketchbook until the design of the object overwhelms him with the wonder of natural law: "At last, the tree was there, and everything that I had thought about trees, nowhere." Occasionally the shattering revelation, like that which effects his deconversion at Turin, involves a group of converging impressions prompted by long-accumulating but hitherto carefully suppressed feelings: the revulsion from the solemn black-coated evangelical preacher in the Waldensian chapel, the delight in seeing a tousled girl of ten basking like a snake in unselfconscious sensuality on a sand heap, the discovery of beauty in the vital voluptuous paganism of Veronese's "Solomon and the Queen of Sheba" in the Royal Gallery—all the contrasts between the self-righteous inhibition he has long been required to cherish and the free assertion of life he has been taught to fear. But the epiphanies of *Praeterita* for the most part are not sequential; they tend to validate a sensibility rather than to further its development. After the childhood chapters Ruskin's method is less chronological than associative and thematic. His ideas, he admits, may have shifted somewhat over the years, and he sets no great store by mere consistency. But he denies that his real self has changed in any essential over the fifty years since he was eighteen.[43] The "total of me," he would have us believe, remains fixed and substantial, still "curious" perhaps, but as timeless as his clearest intimations of a world beyond time.

The last page of *Praeterita* leaves Ruskin in a continuous present, suffering illusions and delusions he would not have thought possible, confusing the receded past with the terrain near at hand, speaking of his dead Rose La Touche as if she were alive and in active correspondence with him. He who once rightly valued his gift of objective analysis sinks into a rambling subjectivity, heedless of logic and coherence. Yet something of his power animates even the last dictated sentence, a vivid evocation of an unreal evening light over Siena with "the fireflies everywhere in the sky and cloud rising and falling, mixed with the lightning, and more intense than the stars." The autobiography has finally become a direct transcript of the self in decline rather than a controlled self-portrait, but a stronger and more characteristic sensibility still flashes with intermittent brilliance across the darkness.

Though temperamentally quite unlike Ruskin and often diametrically opposed to his views, John Stuart Mill as autobiographer was also, nonetheless, in the succession of

Wordsworth—responsive to the subjective impulse, which he believed Wordsworth and the Romantics had first thoroughly explored and validated. Drilled from childhood in an eighteenth-century rationalism and taught to regard Jeremy Bentham as his exemplar, Mill came at the time of his own mental crisis to look upon Bentham as old-fashioned and inadequate, altogether deficient in modern self-consciousness, "that daemon," as he called it, "of the men of genius of our time, from Wordsworth to Byron, from Goethe to Chateaubriand, and to which this age owes so much both of its cheerful and its mournful wisdom."[44] Bentham's lot, he explained, "was cast in a generation of the leanest and barrenest men whom England had yet produced, and he was an old man when a better race came in with the present century." From Wordsworth especially Mill learned to respect what Benthamism had neglected, the internal culture of the feelings and the power of "tranquil contemplation."

Not all self-scrutiny, however, seemed as reassuring as Wordsworth's. The one sort of self-consciousness that Bentham did recognize was self-interest, the individual's "calculus of hedonism," his gauging of the relative proportions of pleasure and pain involved in any given act. Mill, on the other hand, in revulsion from a naive Benthamism, concluded that happiness could not be deliberately willed or secured by conscious striving, but must instead come unawares as a product of self-forgetting. Before long he recognized his own position as close to "the antiselfconsciousness theory of Carlyle," propounded most emphatically in *Sartor Resartus*. Eventually he moved from a close, if uneasy, friendship with Carlyle to a serious estrangement. Yet he seems never to have rejected the message of *Sartor*, and his *Autobiography* is perhaps best understood as a replication of Teufelsdröckh's spiritual progress, which for many of the great Victorians set the standard pattern of conversion.[45]

Sartor postulates three stages of development. Teufels-dröckh first finds himself committed by a prevailing skeptical rationalism to the Everlasting No, the creation, he assumes, of the materialistic eighteenth century, and he wanders through a dreary urban wasteland, devoid of all hope, purpose, and vital principle. At length, however, in the depths of suicidal despair, appropriately in "the dirty little *Rue Saint-Thomas de l'Enfer*," he receives the sudden irrational fiery illumination, the sense of a stubborn residuary free will, rising now strong enough to reject the compulsions of the deterministic No and to carry him to the cool and becalming Centre of Indifference. There he achieves a new perspective on himself and society at large and an intimation that all true living somehow escapes conditioned response and anxious self-interest. He is then prepared to move on to the Everlasting Yea, which will bring a positive reappraisal of his past experience and a dedication to his future work.

Mill's *Autobiography* has a similar tripartite structure, functioning as a sort of Hegelian dialectic. The thesis, constituting the first four chapters, is the strenuous loveless education of the prodigy, presided over by James Mill, and the apprenticeship at sixteen of the philosophic Radical with little feeling and great intellectual zeal. But when the intellect ceases to be all-satisfying and the Utilitarian program no longer seems an all-sufficient happy prospect, the whole thesis becomes an Everlasting No, to be repudiated by "an irrepressible self-consciousness" dissatisfied with the status of "a mere reasoning machine." The "mental crisis" (surely as much emotional as mental) described in Chapter V is the antithesis, the Centre of Indifference at which Mill questions the values of his first phase. Here he discovers an unsuspected capacity for tears, as he reads Marmontel, an unfamiliar response to the passion of Byron and the meditation of Wordsworth, and a quite defiant sympathy with Carlyle, Coleridge, and the new schools of idealism. "The influences of European, that is to say, Continental thought, and especially those of the reaction of the nineteenth century against the eighteenth, were now," he writes, "streaming in upon me."[46] From the collision of thesis and antithesis develops the synthesis presented in the last two chapters, the Everlasting Yea, which, under the auspices of Harriet Taylor Mill, seeks to harmonize the best of Benthamism and the wisdom of a "better," more self-conscious generation and so to establish the sanction for the mature work of the foremost Victorian apostle of liberty.

Carlyle apparently detected no similarity between *Sartor* and Mill's "mental history," for he dismissed the latter as "the autobiography of a steam-engine."[47] Yet the very impersonality of Mill's narrative, especially the early "thesis" chapters, is part of its appeal, even its pathos, to readers distressed to imagine a gifted child denied any clear identity. As a youth, though unexercised physically, ill-trained in social manners, and inept in all practical affairs, Mill knew himself to be at least twenty-five years ahead of his contemporaries in the factual information he had amassed. But he was allowed no pride in his one great asset, his erudition, for that, he was given to understand, was simply the result of his father's extraordinary instruction rather than any unusual aptitude of his own; he was expected instead to hold "a very humble opinion" of himself. Still, he tells us, "My state of mind was not humility, but neither was it arrogance. I never thought of saying to myself, I am, or I can do, so and so. I neither estimated myself highly nor lowly; I did not estimate myself at all."[48] The *Autobiography* is more than the record of a remarkable education, which is its declared intention; it is also, and more significantly, the chronicle of a search for the self, a self suppressed and nerveless till nervous collapse in late adolescence, but then rebellious and sensitive to alien feelings and impressions, and thereafter bolder, more individual, confident in a reasonableness guided by broadened human sympathies. For the mental crisis that leads to such momentous self-discovery, Mill briefly invokes a metaphoric idiom, the language of feeling he had been taught to distrust: the subversive but liberating self-questioning occurs in "the dry heavy dejection of the melancholy winter" when "the fountains of vanity and ambition seemed to have dried up within" him.[49] Whatever Carlyle's opinion, the imagery is reminiscent of the desert in *Sartor* and so a secular equivalent of the "spiritual dryness" in the dark night that traditionally precedes the awakening of the soul.

Late in life, revisiting places he had known as a child, John Henry Newman paused beneath the windows of an old house where, when very young, he had watched from his bed flickering candles set out on the sills to celebrate the victory of Trafalgar. "I have" he wrote, "never seen the house since September 1807. I know more about it than any house I have been in since, and could pass an examination on it. It has been ever in my dreams."[50] Such sharp personal detail is characteristic of the reminiscences of Ruskin or Darwin, but hardly representative of Mill's "mental history," or indeed of Newman's.

The memory in fact is recorded not in his *Apologia pro Vita sua* but in a private letter to a close friend. The *Apologia* reveals acute powers of recall, the ability to reproduce every subtle twist and turn of controversy and every shade of deepening conviction, but it maintains a high degree of reticence, a refusal to explore aspects of subjective experience unrelated to its immediate purpose. Though it insistently defends the role of subjectivity in the assent to faith, it shows no concern with the dreams of a lost childhood or with other personal data, out of which most autobiographies are largely made.

Newman's *Apologia* is first of all what its subtitle of 1873 promises, "A History of his Religious Opinions," his lucid and sharply focused reply not only to Charles Kingsley but to all others who questioned the course of his religious development and the validity of his final religious position. Its narrative, though enriched with the precise and appropriate imagery of a prose master, has no cause to present "images" or vignettes of the individual life apart from its religious commitment. The character of the apologist is to be deduced from the style, tone, and logic of his argument.

Newman was aware, however, that his biographers would demand something more, some further information of a nonreligious kind. Accordingly about ten years after the *Apologia* he prepared an "Autobiographical Memoir," tracing his academic career to the age of thirty, as a model, he thought, of "the simplicity of style in which he desired that all told about himself should be composed." Written, like *The Education of Henry Adams*, in the third person, the "Memoir" is almost as discreet and selective as the *Apologia*. It passes over Newman's childhood without comment except for an indication of the schoolboy's quickness at learning and his distaste for organized games. But it offers some new insight into the college years. Newman's real life apparently begins at Oxford, but it is a life earnest and austere, having no patience with undergraduate frivolities, repelled by the alcoholic exuberance of gaudy-days. His shy self-consciousness at first is extreme; he suffers much from "the recollection of solecisms, whether actual or imagined," in his social conduct. He is grievously disappointed at degree time by his failure to achieve the high academic standing he has expected. But he nonetheless recovers confidence in his intelligence and analytic powers, and he is finally pleased to remember Dr. Whately's compliment that "he was the clearest-headed man he knew." April 12, 1822, which brings his election as a Fellow of Oriel, is "the turning point of his life, and of all days most memorable."[51] Despite academic disputes and differences in the next eight years—or perhaps indeed because of them, for he thrives on intellectual argument—Oxford seems to him his proper home and haven, and he is content to compare himself, in a verse riddle, to the snapdragon clinging to the college walls, unable to imagine any other habitat so lofty or congenial.[52] But such effusions are rare; Mr. Newman, as he calls himself throughout the "Memoir," expounds his principles but for the most part withholds his sentiments.

The *Apologia* in its final form makes repeated disclaimers that the author enjoys in any way the act of self-revelation. The preface declares, "It is not at all pleasant for me to be egotistical; nor to be criticized for being so. It is not pleasant to reveal to high and low, young and old, what has gone on within me from my early years. It is not pleasant to be giving to every shallow or flippant disputant the advantage over me of knowing my most private thoughts, I might even say, the intercourse between myself and my Maker."[53] Successive chapters begin with similar denials. The first suggests the value of privacy, "*Secretum meum mihi.*" Chapter II advises the reader, who may have found some excitement in the account of Newman's return from the Continent in July 1833, that there is in fact "no romantic story to tell," that is to say, no colorful confession to follow. Chapter III, the shortest in time-span but the most crucial in terms of the religious odyssey, solicits our sympathy for the reluctant autobiographer, who must perform on himself "a cruel operation, the ripping up of old griefs." Of all bold ventures he has ever undertaken, Newman avers, "this is the boldest," the self-explanation essential if he is to convince us of his reasonableness and probity. Chapter IV, describing in painful self-scrutiny the waning of his Anglicanism, may, he fears, be simply a long death-bed scene of "little interest" to his readers; its method, at any rate, he adds, must be solidly factual and documentary. Only with the fifth and final chapter, the account of his Catholic years, does he feel absolved of the burden of self-exposure, and only then, paradoxically, is he free to be most passionately personal.

The drama of the *Apologia* lies in the clash of ideas held with intense emotion. We observe the workings of Newman's mind, but we see little of the human being, the body in a visualized setting such as Wordsworth or Ruskin present. Two passages from the first chapter, however, attract attention by specific novelistic detail. The first of these records, briefly but warmly, what amounts to a spot of time, "that hour fixed in my memory after the changes of forty-two years, forty-two this very day on which I write": the occasion of his being summoned to the tower of Oriel, on his election as a Fellow, to meet the saintly John Keble, and his sudden overwhelming sense of unworthiness to receive Keble's congratulatory handshake.

The second and considerably longer break from the regular analytic style describes Newman's Italian journey and his illness in Sicily, in terms that invite comparison with Mill's narrative of his mental crisis and also with the dialectic of *Sartor Resartus*. The traveler senses "some inward changes" coming upon him. He is distressed by the condition of the English Church and unresponsive to the Roman. He admires Italian scenery and historic landmarks but cares nothing for the Italian people; he is isolated, lonely, more and more "driven back" into himself, perplexed rather than desperate, yet sharing Byron's view (which he quotes) that here, under the Mediterranean sun, "All, save the spirit of man is divine." He is now as close as he could come to an Everlasting No. At Castro-Giovanni he suffers physical collapse, but in semidelirium he murmurs, "I shall not die, for I have not sinned against light, I have not sinned against light"—the precise meaning of which eludes him, though the words, we might now say, imply the rejection of despair and, in terms of the pattern of *Sartor*, the transition to a Centre of Indifference. Gradually recovering, he finds release—as the young Mill did—in tears and in new resolution:

Before starting from my inn in the morning of May 26th or 27th, I sat down on my bed, and began to sob violently. My servant, who had acted as my nurse, asked what ailed me. I could only answer him, "I have a work to do in England."[54]

The work in England proves to be Newman's Everlasting Yea, a strenuous mission, extending for more than a decade, through which he discovers his gifts of leadership and persuasion and virtually his personal identity.

The three chapters devoted to the course of the Oxford Movement then revert to a mode of intellectual analysis, which largely excludes circumstantial private detail. At the end of his spiritual journey, when he finally abandons the Anglican Church, he is deeply distressed to take leave of his college. But he expresses his feeling obliquely, invoking the snapdragon of his early poem, which was, he says, to have been the "emblem" of his permanent attachment to the University.

Though entitled "Position of my Mind since 1845," the
conclusion of the *Apologia* is concerned in the main with
two larger issues: the general cogency of Catholic dogma
and the conduct of the Catholic priesthood. In discussing
the latter, Newman descends of necessity to the level of the
pragmatic, with the result that his defense of the practice
of casuistry and equivocation reads at times like a specious
rationalizing of expediency. On the other hand, when propounding matters of dogma, he rises to a great personal
intensity, for he wholly identifies the Catholic faith with
his own spiritual perception and commitment. No passage
in autobiography since St. Augustine's meditation on time
and eternity surpasses Newman's impassioned description
of the consequences of "original sin," his tremendous catalogue of mankind's errors and miseries, inspiring "a vision
to dizzy and appal" and to inflict "upon the mind the sense
of a profound tragedy which is absolutely beyond human
solution." For Newman there is no sufficient stay against
despair and infidelity in all the "objective" world of nature.
The saving faith must come from within, from a "voice,
speaking so clearly in my conscience and my heart," which
makes "the being of a God . . . as certain to me as the
certainty of my own existence." God, who is to be reached
subjectively, is in turn the guarantor of the subjective life.
"If I looked into a mirror," Newman writes, "and did not
see my own face, I should have the sort of feeling which
actually comes upon me, when I look into the living busy
world, and see no reflexion of its Creator."[55] To Newman
the familiar analogy of the mirror has acquired a new vitality; both faces are indeed realities; religious faith must
transcend what confuses human reason and logic, the apparent disjunction between Creator and creation. Whatever
its first purpose as a limited and more or less impersonal

autobiography, the *Apologia pro Vita sua* stands in final effect as something more, as Newman's profession of a faith which is the very sanction of his selfhood.

Insofar as he could relate his own subjectivity to a solidly objective Church, Newman considered Wordsworth's undirected subjective impulse, vague and ill-grounded, essentially secular yet spuriously religious. Wordsworth was to be valued, he thought, as a poet of "philosophic meditation," representative of the mind of the age, but at the same time to be rebuked for his "almost sacerdotal pretensions."[56] Others, however, unable to achieve Newman's complete assent to Christian dogma, saw in Wordsworth's inwardness a substitute religion or at least "the illustration or embodiment of some spiritual law."[57] Among these, William Hale White, through his persona "Mark Rutherford," left, I think, the most striking late-Victorian testimony of indebtedness.

Repelled by the ignorance and narrow fundamentalism of a theological school, where he is in training as a Dissenting minister, Mark Rutherford comes unexpectedly upon a copy of the *Lyrical Ballads*, and the discovery proves a more than Wordsworthian spot of time, "a day I remember as well as Paul must have remembered afterwards the day on which he went to Damascus," for "the change it wrought in me could only be compared with that which is said to have been wrought on Paul himself by the Divine apparition." The precise cause of his response to the volume remains elusive, but the effect is decided and dramatic:

it excited a movement and a growth which went on till, by degrees, all the systems which enveloped me like a body gradually decayed from me and fell away into nothing. Of more importance, too, than the decay of systems was the birth of a habit of inner reference and a dislike to occupy myself with anything which did not in some way or other touch the soul. . . . Wordsworth unconsciously did for me what every religious reformer has done,—he re-created my Supreme Divinity; substituting a new and living spirit for the old deity, once alive, but gradually hardened into an idol.[58]

But if it liberalizes—or liberates—his faith, Mark Rutherford's new "habit of inner reference" offers no permanent solution to his deepest misgivings. His introspection engenders a fear of the self and for the self. He experiences a loneliness far less creative than Wordsworth's solitude. He shyly retreats from society but yearns for companionship and shared understanding. He suffers a recurrent intense hypochondria, a shattering mistrust of his own physical being. Eventually he is to be saved only by accepting what is good in the present and setting aside his dread of the future and all hopeless metaphysical questioning. Yet he cannot entirely forgo speculation, for he knows that such sacrifice can be achieved only at the expense of the sensitivity that defines his character.

The Autobiography of Mark Rutherford, for all its probing self-revelation, remains a modest and diffident book, the product of a latterday Puritan, a self-history in the tradition of Bunyan, set like *Grace Abounding* in nonconformist Bedford. Its first page apologizes for the whole as "a record of weakness and failures" and "the tale of a commonplace life" but suggests that the story nonetheless may have some value as the description of early-Victorian Dissent. White, like Bunyan the master of a quiet middle style, has no desire for self-advertisement. He not only conceals himself behind the mask of Rutherford; he also devises an epilogue in which an unidentified friend expresses some fear that the reader may think Rutherford "a mere egoist, selfish and self-absorbed."[59] No one who has followed the simple, unadorned narrative from the beginning will find much cause to pass that judgment.

Few twentieth-century autobiographers discover in Wordsworth the grounds of a new religion, and still fewer retrace the high-Victorian progress from despair to a triumphant, unequivocal Everlasting Yea. But, if vigorous assertion is no longer the mode, the possibility of spiritual or psychological change is still a central concern, and the spot of time remains an experience to respect and remember. As in *The Prelude*, the self, at least as presented in the most compelling personal histories, still seeks in the ordinary world of sense and outward things the source of extraordinary vision, the momentary glimpse—beyond all reasonable expectation—of meaning, coherence, or direction.

Bertrand Russell's brilliant, disjointed autobiography was the late and relatively casual byproduct of the longest life vouchsafed to any British philosopher. As autobiographer Russell keeps moving away from self-portraiture to descriptions of his encounters with the intellectual community; he combines personal narrative with a varied correspondence, and after the first of three volumes he relies perhaps too heavily on the latter. But he offers us, nonetheless, a remarkable impression of a curious temperament, the mind of a rationalist whose faith and conduct repeatedly defy logic and reason. He makes crucial decisions on sudden impulse. In his first volume, covering his first forty-two years, he records several intuitions, some less edifying than his reaction to Mrs. Whitehead's seizure. He tells of reading Mill's *Autobiography* at the age of eighteen, lingering over one particular sentence, and becoming forthwith a confirmed atheist. With cool dispassion he reports the discovery of trouble in his first marriage: "I went out bicycling one afternoon, and suddenly, as I was riding along a country road, I realized that I no longer loved Alys. I had had no idea until this moment that my love for her was even lessening. The problem presented by this discovery was very grave." Ten years later, in March 1911, the same capricious vehicle provides sudden and complete escape: having given Alys's niece a lesson in philosophy, "I then rode away on my bicycle, and with that my first marriage came to an end. I did not see Alys again till 1950, when we met as friendly acquaintances."[60]

Russell's prose can be as direct and incisive as its content. The style throughout his self-history proclaims the man, disarmingly candid, yet too abrupt in disclosure, and so oddly reticent, brooking no question, self-justifying, arrogant, and assured, by turns self-absorbed and wittily detached from self-regard. His "epiphanies," relating erratically to his own practical affairs, reach for no metaphysical values or Wordsworthian "types and symbols of eternity." Yet his declared preference for the temporal does not preclude a strain of poetry, a nostalgia for the fixed abiding past, which brings him close to self-contradiction, a denial of eternality but at the same time a half-mystical intimation of some timeless order. "Yes," he tells a friend,

one must learn to live in the Past, and so to dominate it that it is not a disquieting ghost or a horrible gibbering spectre stalking through the vast bare halls that were once full of life, but a gentle soothing companion, reminding one of the possibility of good things, and rebuking cynicism and cruelty. . . . For my part, I do not even wish to live rather with eternal things, though I often give them lip-service; but in my heart I believe that the best things are those that are fragile and temporary, and I find a magic in the Past which eternity cannot possess. Besides, nothing is more eternal than the Past—the present and future are still subject to Time, but the Past has escaped into immortality—Time has done his worst, and it yet lives.[61]

Hungry for eternity as Russell was not, C. S. Lewis acknowledged a direct, unembarrassed debt to the Romantic tradition. *Surprised by Joy* (1935), the title from one of Wordsworth's sonnets, announces by its subtitle, "The Shape of my Early Life," the concern of *The Prelude* with childhood, youth, dedication, and memory. A selective narrative of Lewis's first thirty years, culminating in his conversion to Christianity, the autobiography, like Wordsworth's, places its spiritual affirmation in a closely observed ordinary world. Lewis clearly evokes the circumstances of the child's life in his unaesthetic, unimaginative Northern Irish home, the lonely drab misery of his terms at an English public school, and always the longing that both places engendered for some absent principle of beauty. He remembers the precise settings of his moments of revelation and decision, his spots of time, a stillness of mind snatched from physical motion: the color of sky and field seen from a train on the evening he discovered the visionary power of George MacDonald's romance, *Phantastes;* the ride atop a bus up Headington Hill when he reluctantly surrendered his atheism; the drive to Whipsnade during which he recognized the direction of his religious commitment.

The Joy that Lewis celebrates is not the attained faith but the earlier recurrent "inconsolable longing" for a dimension of life beyond our commonplace routine, the stab, the sudden sharp sense of loss and deprivation. As the yearning rather than the fulfillment, Joy is "an unsatisfied desire which is itself more desirable than any other satisfaction." It comes by surprise, the byproduct of self-forgetfulness, and cannot be deliberately sought or cultivated, though its quality may be suggested by engaged response to music or literature. Joy to Lewis may be the memory of a memory, the recollection of a time when the yearning was all-possessive, as, for example, a frosty hill walk, just after receiving the Christmas gift of Wagner's *Ring*, remembered as a time of anticipated great pleasure in reading—"It seemed to me that I had tasted heaven then."[62] Wordsworth, he concludes, was mistaken in lamenting the passing of a glory, the loss of vision, for the very wanting was itself the having, and *The Prelude* as a whole realizes the desire by giving it expression.[63] Ultimately, however, Lewis himself comes to consider Joy less important as something achieved than as the evidence of a deeper subjective need. With his conversion, at the end of his narrative, that need is satisfied by a faith less vague and transitory than sudden hunger, and Joy in itself then ceases to be the central object of desire.

Edwin Muir had as deep a religious sense as Lewis and by the end as firm a Christian commitment, though no comparable concern with dogmatic theology. But his *Autobiography*, in its first form called *The Story and the Fable*, is neither a narrative of conversion nor an essay in apologetics.[64] It quietly presents the essential outlines of a modern poet's career and the development of his gentle yet acute sensibility.

The "story" is the record of events and things, the man's year-by-year progress in the "ordinary" world (for the "ordinary" is as much Muir's point of departure as it was Wordsworth's). The book, like Ruskin's *Praeterita*, is arranged according to places of residence and work; and the physical settings—the Orkney island farm of his infancy, the slums of Glasgow, the fetid bone factory at Fairport, literary London, subverted Prague—are all observed and delineated with a Ruskinian precision. From the beginning, however, there beckons a dimension beyond common measurement. "The Orkney I was born into," Muir writes, "was a place where there was no great distinction between the ordinary and the fabulous, the lives of living men turned into legend."[65] On the mainland of his maturity, where the distinction was often sharp indeed, Muir continued to seek out the fabulous.

The "fable" relates to a large elusive subjectivity, encompassing and transcending the finite life in time. As autobiographer Muir faces the problem of how to know and define the self; for each man, he believes, draws on the aggregate experience of mankind, somehow absorbs the myths and archetypes postulated by Jung, and so shares in some vast collective consciousness. Though Muir finally sees no single "neat pattern" in his own life, on the way he has had salutary glimpses of meaning and coherence. The mature disposal of a childish fear brings him such satisfying reassurance, "an unsolicited act of help where no help was known to be":

These solutions of the past projected into the present, deliberately announced as if they were a sybilline declaration that life has a meaning, impress me more deeply than any other kind of experience with the conviction that life does have a meaning quite apart from the thousand meanings which the conscious mind attributes to it: an unexpected and yet incontestable meaning which runs in the teeth of ordinary experience, perfectly coherent, yet depending on a different system of connected relations from that by which we consciously live.[66]

One of these primitive unexpressed relations that haunts Muir's imagination is man's kinship with the animals, and one of his recurrent discomforts is his sense of blood guilt for the betrayal of the animal order. Yet he dreads more intensely the degradation of human beings to the bestial level. In his most frightening spot of time he suffers a sudden hallucination which transforms all his fellow-passengers

on a Glasgow tramcar into pigs and then extends the vision
to a whole world of "nothing but millions of such creatures
living an animal life and moving towards an animal death
as towards a great slaughter-house." Images of like intensity
recur in Muir's troubled dreams and nightmares, presented
like De Quincey's in circumstantial detail, but offered here
by one who has read Freud and has sought release in Freudian interpretation and analysis from deadly fears and traumas. Not all of his "fabling," however, partakes of neurosis
or demands clinical exorcism; his more positive intuitions,
as he describes them, elude altogether the reductive expla-
nations of his therapist, who wishes, understandably, to
reinstate the rational, the normal, and the "ordinary."

Muir's psychology, happily free of latterday jargon, derives as much from Wordsworth as from Freud, and his
autobiography, expressing some direct debt but far greater
Romantic affinity, provides the strongest modern witness
to the persistence of the method and concern of *The Prelude.*
Muir, like Wordsworth, recognizes the power and indeed
the sanctity of memory as a warrant of selfhood and purpose. His review of the past—both in this present book and
earlier at a crucial stage of his career, when he perceived
his true vocation as poet—brings a sense of long misdirected
effort and a new perspective. "In living that life over again,"
he writes, "I struck up a first acquaintance with myself."[67]
Looking backwards, he escapes the "order to time" and the
forward rush of temporal things. He recovers his childhood
assumption of timelessness, of living in an infinite universe,
and his first intimations of immortality.[68] With renewed
confidence he comes to regard his real life as more durable
and less restricted than the fixed personality that ordinary
routine has impressed upon him, to realize, as he puts it,
"that immortality is not an idea or a belief, but a state of

being in which man keeps alive in himself his perception of that boundless union and freedom, which he can faintly apprehend in time, though its consummation lies beyond time."[69]

As in Wordsworth and indeed in all the major autobiographers, the "fable" ultimately counts for more than the "story." Muir has pleasures as well as miseries to record— the achievement, for example, of a happy marriage. But he chooses to tell us little of his personal affairs, for his interest in reviewing the past lies in the quality of the life he has experienced and not in a factual record of private circumstance. Unlike popular memoirists, he seeks no reflected glory from accounts of the many celebrities he must surely have known in England or during his long years abroad. The one friend he especially honors is John Holms, a man of unfulfilled renown. Holms, he declares, was the "most remarkable" person he ever met, because the least self-conscious, "not a personality" at all, but simply a "nature," a power of pure intellect and emotion.[70] Muir himself, selfless in his self-probing, was apparently, as he quite inadvertently suggests, such an impersonal natural force. Yet it may seem something of a paradox that his autobiography, one of the most profoundly subjective since *The Prelude*, points to the conquest, rather than the cultivation, of distinctive personality as the highest human aspiration.

‹§ V §›

INVENTED SELVES

And we have been on many thousand lines,
And we have shown, on each, spirit and power;
But hardly have we, for one little hour
Been on our own line, have we been ourselves.
—*Matthew Arnold*

Fascinated by the masks he could fashion for himself, Yeats praised Oscar Wilde's ability to strike an unconventional pose, to sustain the "discipline" of a new role,
and to observe public reaction to his performance. Wordsworth by contrast, he argued, was "often flat and heavy"
because he had "no theatrical element" in his character but
simply "an obedience to a discipline which he [had] not
created."[1]

Setting aside the value judgment, we might apply Yeats's
comment specifically to *The Prelude* and extend it to other
nineteenth-century self-presentations. We might then agree
that Wordsworth and the major Victorian autobiographers,
however dramatic may have been their sense of discovery
and commitment, however resourceful their rhetorical strategies, were all indeed untheatrical. Each, to be sure, recognized his role in life and played it effectively: Wordsworth
as the dedicated poet, Darwin as the scientific observer,
Ruskin as the critical spectator, Newman as religious leader,
Mill as defender of intellectual liberty. But each assumed

his role as something given by endowment, circumstance, and vocation, rather than as a part he himself was devising and staging for special effect. The question of sincerity in their autobiographies scarcely arises, for by the time of reviewing their careers, each of them had supplied ample objective evidence that the role claimed was his true and sufficient identity.

In the more "theatrical" late-Victorian generation, on the other hand, the author of a self-history was less confident of the truths of selfhood, and his self-presentation, or role-playing, involved a different sort of self-consciousness. Though acutely aware of his audience, he felt alienated from the ordinary world and no longer accountable to it. "The egoistic note," Wilde remarked in 1897, "is, . . . and always has been to me, the primal and ultimate note of modern art, but *to be an Egoist one must have an Ego.*"[2] The "personality," in other words, as opposed to the "nature" of a man that Edwin Muir would prize,[3] must validate itself by the uniqueness of private impressions and the individuality of personal style, the singularity of gesture and voice. If the self as a separate entity seemed elusive and amorphous, or if it, perhaps, did not exist at all, it must be invented, dressed up, and projected. It mattered little that the creation of a self-image might distort the masker's actual experience or willfully commingle fiction with fact.

In the most striking late-Victorian autobiography Wilde himself rehearsed his boldest role. Though written as a letter from Reading Gaol and first published in full more than sixty years later, *De Profundis* reads like a long carefully wrought monologue in an immediate cultural tragedy. Lord Alfred Douglas, the addressee, is cast as the ruthless self-seeking antagonist who precipitates the hero's downfall; and many pages denounce his perfidy. But the letter must transcend diatribe, must destroy all bitterness of heart; it should prove, Wilde insists, "as important a crisis and turning-point" in Douglas's life as "the writing of it" proves in Wilde's own. The writer, the speaker, is, of course, the real subject, the actor at center stage. At frequent intervals he reminds us of his tragic credentials, of the greatness he has lost or betrayed. He declares himself the scion of a noble and honored family, the master of every literary form he touched, "once a lord of language," an incomparable shaper of public thought and feeling: "The gods had given me almost everything. I had genius, a distinguished name, high social position, brilliancy, intellectual daring."[4] For every good reason, then, "I was a man who stood in symbolic relations to the art and culture of my age. I had realised this for myself at the very dawn of my manhood, and had forced my age to realise it afterwards."[5] Now that he has fallen, though he may revile Douglas, he must recognize the real tragic flaw in himself, since "nobody, great or small, can be ruined except by his own hand."[6] Henceforth he must practice deep humility. The model he chooses in his grief is Christ, the Man of Sorrows, whom he refashions quite arbitrarily in his own image as the "artist in sympathy," the arch-individualist, the first Romantic, and the determined anti-Philistine. When released from prison, he will, he vows, go down to the sea for healing and a new baptism—he remembers Euripides' saying that the sea "washes away the stains and sins of the world." There Nature, he trusts, or at least fantasizes, will restore him: "She will hang the night with stars so that I may walk abroad in the darkness without stumbling, and send the wind over my footprints so that none may track me to my hurt; she will cleanse me in great waters, and with bitter herbs make me whole."[7]

Whether or not, as Wilde once remarked, "one should always be a little improbable," the prose of *De Profundis* as here is often implausible, derivative, and self-indulgent. The actor himself is scarcely persuaded by his rhetorical compunction, and he can hardly expect his audience to be. In an earlier passage of confessed abasement, concluding with a quotation from one of his own plays, he declares, "I would not a bit mind sleeping in the cool grass in summer, and when winter came on sheltering myself by the warm close-thatched rick, or under the penthouse of a great barn, provided I had love in my heart. The external things of life seem to me now of no importance at all. You can see to what intensity of individualism I have arrived, or am ar-riving rather, for the journey is long, and 'where I walk there are thorns.' "[8] But the aesthetic, urban self-image he has presented throughout his career is too strong for him— or for us—to take his rural excursion seriously, and he at once seeks refuge in a self-conscious, ironic realism: "Of course I know that to ask for alms on the highway is not to be my lot, and that if ever I lie in the cool grass at night-time it will be to write sonnets to the Moon."[9]

Nonetheless, despite splashes of false sentiment, Wilde seems truly to mean much of what he says. If his claim to honored family is somewhat shaken by what we know of his raffish parents, his estimate of his own literary prowess is not wholly unjustified. By virtue of *The Importance of Being Earnest* and *Intentions*, his achievement both as writer of comedy and as critic is unassailable. He was, indeed, as most cultural historians now see him, the representative man of letters of the English 'nineties. And fallen from his brief eminence, he did suffer cruelly for his indiscretion and folly. Few descriptions of humiliation could be more moving than his account of standing handcuffed, in con-

spicuous prison garb, for half an hour on the central plat-
form at Clapham Junction, while successive trains poured
forth a jeering mob.

But our sympathy wavers as soon as he shifts his rhetoric
to extravagant hyperbole or precious metaphor, when he
recalls his majesty as King of "that beautiful unreal world
of Art" or strives to reproduce not just his sorrow but "the
purple pageant of [his] incommunicable woe."[10] At such
moments the actor's mask is more apparent than the reality
of the self behind it; we begin to wonder what sort of Ego,
if any at all, the Egoist actually has. By the end, however,
the jarring lines count for less than the virtuoso performance; we come to see the role as an act of courage, the
necessary protection of a hurt self against a demeaning pity.

For most of his private life, lived as it was largely in
public, Wilde avoided self-confrontation. To be sure, he
had his own special insights, his "spots of time," and he
even borrowed directly from Wordsworth when he discussed the problem of sustaining such vision: "One can
realise a thing in a single moment, but one loses it in the
long hours that follow with leaden feet. It is so difficult to
keep 'heights that the soul is competent to gain.' "[11] But he
dreaded revealing the long dull stretches of commonplace
routine, the emptiness of the "ordinary" Wordsworthian
perception. In his art he repeatedly invoked epigram and
apothegm to generalize or dismiss his personal experience,
and abundant defensive wit to conceal his unruly sentiment.
Some months after his release from Reading Gaol, once
more seeking an adequate mask but now finding none, he
wryly remarked, "A man's face is his autobiography; a
woman's face is her work of fiction."[12] In his most characteristic writing from the beginning through De Profundis
he himself made no great distinction between the two
genres.

George Moore, with a less immediate need for dramatic gesture, also created fictions of the self. At least eight of his books belong to the autobiographical mode as he conceived it, an amalgam of incident, impression, and invention, commingling records of private life, sometimes embarrassingly frank, often heightened or distorted, with long stretches of confident art criticism and much literary gossip, all calculated to demonstrate his intelligence, sophistication, and importance.

Moore's motivation as perpetual autobiographer is most apparent in his trilogy, *Hail and Farewell,* where he claims to have been woefully neglected by parents who from his early childhood persuaded him of his personal ugliness, incompetence, and stupidity. He is quite aware that he may have overcompensated for his "inveterate belief in [his] own inferiority." Nonetheless, he insists, "Within the oftentimes bombastic and truculent appearance that I present to the world, trembles a heart shy as a wren in the hedgerow or a mouse along the wainscoting."[13] His swaggering bravado, then, which the Yeats circle dismissed with contempt, was simply the "theatrical element" in a deliberate and often desperate self-assertion that Yeats elsewhere applauded.

Moore's first and most flamboyant self-advertisement, *Confessions of a Young Man,* published in 1888, exploits some of the materials treated rather more discreetly in his later autobiographies but offers no explanation for the young man's rebellious behavior. The confessor is ostensibly one Edward Dayne, but the disguise is very thin; the author seems uncertain whether his first name is Edward or Edouard or Edwin (he uses all three forms), and in the French edition of 1889 he drops the alias altogether and calls himself George Moore. His inspiration, he says, is St. Augustine, but whereas that great exemplar told "the story of a God-tortured soul," he intends to tell for the first time "the story of an art-tortured soul."[14] He accordingly creates and maintains the pose of an expatriated aesthete living in Paris, producing no art but talking endlessly about it and enjoying the ambiance of artists. Even the possibility of a foolish duel poses no serious threat to his determined dilettantism: "We went out to dinner, we went to the theatre, and after the theatre we went home and aestheticised till three in the morning"; or, as a revised version reads, "After the theatre we went home and aestheticized till the duel became the least important event and Marshall's picture the greatest."[15]

The young man's opinions are expected to dismay and repel the respectable reader. Declaring himself bored with the "decencies of life," Dayne, or Moore, boasts of his faults and foibles, his willful hedonism and monstrous dissipations. He toys with sadistic emotion and the idea of decadence. He avows an "appetite for the strange, abnormal and unhealthy in art." He alleges "feminine depravities in his affections":

I am feminine, morbid, perverse. But above all perverse, almost everything perverse interests, fascinates me. Wordsworth is the only simple-minded man I ever loved, if that great austere mind, chill even as the Cumberland year, can be called simple.[16]

But he has, of course, none of Wordsworth's concern for the common man or the "ordinary sight." The pyramids, he contends, were well worth all the millions of wretched lives sacrificed to build them, if eventually they may "fill a musing hour with wonderment." His literary models, he boasts, are Gautier and Baudelaire, in whom he thinks he finds a defiantly pagan amorality and a rejection of Christian pity, which he himself dismisses as "that most vile of all vile virtues." Looking into the future, he deplores the coming victory of "pity and justice," the light he chooses to call darkness, "which is imminent, which is the twentieth century."[17]

Clearly Moore has no great gift of prophecy, and his flagrant irreligion plumbs no Nietzschean depths, nor carries any real conviction. It is largely an irrelevance, serving only to shock the pious and to sanction his own aesthetic autonomy and his release from moral and social concern. By the end, when his "exquisitely hypocritical reader" is asked, ironically no doubt, to accept the short and fragmentary record as "this long narrative of a sinful life," *Confessions of a Young Man* has become its own parody. Moore obviously prides himself on his wit, daring, and outrageous overstatement. But the part he plays lacks all real intensity; the noisy aesthete, far from being a genuinely art-tortured soul, can scarcely imagine the pains of aesthetic creation.

In his *Confessions* Moore twice disparages Edmund Gosse as the typical Philistine of literature, begotten in a London club by an overstuffed armchair.[18] Nonetheless, the two men remained close friends for nearly forty years, and Moore took credit upon himself[19] for suggesting that Gosse write the personal history that was to prove his most enduring book. Gosse's talent as "objective" novelist, at least as evinced by his one slight romance, was far smaller than Moore's, but his capacity for sustained autobiographical narrative was surely greater. *Father and Son* is a well-shaped chronicle of the self, as "theatrical" in presentation as Yeats could have wished. Begun in the early 'nineties and published anonymously after delays in 1907, it remains the best example of the movement of late nineteenth-century autobiography toward a self-consciously literary form, more intent on dramatic coloring than on verifiable factual accuracy, a genre

ultimately where the author may seem to create a self in
the very act of writing and where his existence in any other
state of being may be questioned or denied.

At the outset of *Father and Son* Gosse warns the reader
that his narrative will blend comedy and tragedy in odd,
perhaps disturbing, proportions. He clearly aims at a tragic
pathos, but he freely employs comic devices, the strategies
of satire and irony, to lend dramatic edge and distance to
his story. He designs the whole as a sort of Bildungsroman
describing his lonely childhood, the restraints imposed upon
him by his father's narrow fundamentalism, and eventually
his liberation at seventeen, when he leaves his home, his
village, and the religious Brethren, to make his independent,
agnostic way in the secular city. As the past unfolds in
sharpened detail, many earnest episodes fall into comic perspective: the child experiments with idolatry by worship-
ping a chair; the child expresses dismay that his widowed
father is about to marry a "pedobaptist"; the father fulmi-
nates against a Christmas pudding as the accursed relic of
pagan ritual; the father prays with the son for guidance to
refuse an invitation to a tea party, and the son rises from
his knees to declare that the Lord has granted him permission to attend; at the party itself the son shocks his audience
by reciting morbid "graveyard" verses he himself only half-
understands. Throughout the narrative minor figures among
the servants and the "Saints" appear with comic height-
ening; the son's governess, Miss Marks, in particular, emerges
as "somewhat grotesque, . . . a kind of Dickens eccentric,
a mixture of Mrs. Pipchin and Miss Sally Brass."[20] But the
"tragic" note intrudes upon the comedy. The boy's mother
dies a sad solemn death, her last gesture dedicating him
irrevocably to the Lord and a life of perfect piety. The
narrator evokes the pathos of the scene but then moves at
once from object to subject, from the dying woman to him-

self and self-pity: "But what a weight," he comments, "intolerable as the burden of Atlas, to lay on the shoulders of a fragile child."[21]

Gosse casts himself as the protagonist of this tragicomedy, the innocent victim of repression driven to subterfuge and deceit in order to preserve his selfhood. Like Mill's *Autobiography*, his narrative describes a rigorous education supervised by a well-meaning parent of sorely limited vision. But the spiritual or intellectual distance between parent and child in Gosse's book is immeasurably greater than in Mill's. Whereas Mill eventually assimilates, deepens, and enriches his father's philosophy, Gosse questions the "Great Scheme" of enforced dedication, comes to repudiate his father's creed as a wholly untenable fanaticism, and sharply dramatizes, in a fashion quite alien to Mill, his escape from stifling commitment. Subtitling his story "A Study of Two Temperaments," he announces in his first sentence that the "struggle," the clash of the two, is to be his theme and that final "disruption" will be the inevitable result of the conflict. As in earlier autobiographies, an epiphany prepares the self for decisive conversion, but here it is deliberately contrived and placed as a climax in a novelistic structure. The son at boarding school, just before beginning his apprenticeship in London, contemplates the setting sun in the hope of a great apocalypse, the Lord's opening of the heavens to carry him off to Paradise. But when no assumption takes place, he is half-ashamed of what he recognizes as a "theatrical attitude," in which perhaps he has never really believed. The anticlimax, at all events, is cruelly crushing:

The tea-bell rang,—the last word of prose to shatter my mystical poetry. "The Lord has not come, the Lord will never come," I muttered, and in my heart the artificial edifice of extravagant faith began to totter and crumble. From that moment forth my Father and I, though the fact was long successfully concealed from him and even from myself, walked in opposite hemispheres of the soul, with "the thick o' the world between us."[22]

The epiphany, whatever its origin in actual experience, has the effect of fiction; the "mystical poetry" invites its immediate ironical reduction to the commonsensical, though still highly literary, "prose."

Throughout his narrative Gosse so molds his materials that they seem less remembered than invented, or at least embellished for the occasion. Nonetheless, he expects us to accept his story as "scrupulously true," in all respects "a genuine slice of life," for, he insists, "this record can . . . have no value that is not based on its rigorous adhesion to the truth."[23] The preface offers us a "document," the "diagnosis of a dying Puritanism," and the text is intended to have large implications, to depict the struggle not just of "two temperaments" and "two consciences" but also of "two epochs." Yet its truth as representative cultural history is debatable. At times it reads like yet another generalized Edwardian indictment of Victorianism. But to most Victorians, who enjoyed a measure of conviviality and folk ritual, including Christmas and plum pudding, the austerities of the Brethren would have seemed eccentric and repulsive. Few Victorian children suffered the son's almost total deprivation of imaginative literature, and no Victorian scientist, as even Gosse admits, was prepared to endorse the father's egregiously theologized biology. For the more convincing aspects of the record we must turn to the uniquely personal relationship between father and son, and even there our estimate of the "truth" will rest on our response to a skillful blend of fact and special pleading.

Father and Son is designed as the son's apologia, his self-defense against intransigent principle. But the unintended irony of the book—its strength as well as its weakness—lies in the possibility that our sympathy may ultimately shift from the son to the father. Whatever his narrowness of view, his literalism, his fear of art and artifice, his misplaced ingenuity in the attempt to forestall the heresies of Darwin, the father remains a strong character, a man of unimpeachable integrity, loyal though mistaken in some of his loyalties, sincerely committed to his faith. He survives the son's descriptions weighted against him, efforts to read his unspoken thoughts, insinuations that he was unduly fond of the sound of his own voice lifted in private prayer or that he delighted in gymnastic gesticulation as he made his devout entreaties. The son by comparison is disingenuous and evasive. When as a youth alone in the city, overcome "by an invincible *ennui*," he breaks his promise to his father to keep up daily Bible readings, he conceals his deception: "The dilemma was now before me that I must either deceive my Father in such things or paralyse my own character."[24] It does not occur to him that another alternative might be possible—the honest disclosure of his own changing attitude. In the long run the father, not deceived, is strong enough in love to forgive. The son, for all his declared devotion to Truth, cares most for his own comfort and his final escape from the burden of "dedication." As a boy he found, he claims, an inner resource: "Through thick and thin I clung to a hard nut of individuality deep down in my childish nature."[25] As a liberated young man he is able at last to exercise "a human being's privilege to fashion his inner life for himself."[26] Of the child's secret resistance, we have indeed some distinct notion. Of the sincerity and strength of the selfhood to be shaped by the liberated adult, we have no such clear assurance.

The Education of Henry Adams, which appeared, privately printed, in the same year as *Father and Son,* records no religious conflict at all comparable to Gosse's and no repudiation of a repressive background. Though uncomfortably aware that much might be expected of him, Adams finds no occasion to proclaim his spiritual independence of a more fully committed father. Nor, on the other hand, does he feel any need to magnify, as Wilde did, his heritage and the social standing of his parents. His early rationality was cool and collected; his credentials of birth and station were impeccable; his position as an Adams was assured. Yet as autobiographer he is in his own way even more "theatrical" than Gosse or Wilde, readier, that is, to assume diverse roles and to fit his life-story into a rigid mold of artifice. Despite an obvious endowment of intellect and sensibility and an unusually wide and privileged view of experience, both in America and abroad, he chooses to consider his "education" a series of melancholy failures and himself its disillusioned product. Wilde in the depths of Reading Gaol remains capable of the brave gesture, never quite so defeated as Adams imagines himself to have been, at liberty, in the highest circles of polite society.

Concentrating on that "education," however broadly he construes the theme, Adams deems himself free to exclude large segments of his career, most conspicuously, perhaps, any reference to his tragic marriage. But the story he tells retains enough variety of setting and observation, travel, episode, and reflection to belie the bleak judgments he has determined to impose upon it. Chapter after chapter, even when animated by incidents and impressions a less jaundiced memory would have cherished, ends with the refrain of failure. Harvard College fails to educate. Berlin disappoints. Rome and Paris offer nothing permanent. Five years in London, crowded with political excitement and social event, prove only "a false start." Washington brings repeated disenchantment. "Failure" labels the account of an apparently successful academic career, followed by a dismal foray into journalism: "Thus it turned out that of all his many educations, Adams thought that of school-teacher the thinnest. Yet he was forced to admit that the education of an editor, in some ways, was thinner still."[27] In spite of a self-protective chilly reserve, he eventually does warm to two close friends, Clarence King and John Hay, both of whom he deems, like himself, undervalued and misunderstood. For the most part, however, personal emotion yields to cold critical appraisal. Unlike Wordsworth or C. S. Lewis, he is never to be "surprised by joy." As "one of his eminent uncles or relations" remarks, even his Class Oration on graduating from Harvard is "singularly wanting in enthusiasm."[28] At the beginning of his narrative he declares his preparation for the game of life and then almost immediately announces his withdrawal: "As it happened, he never got to the point of playing the game at all; he lost himself in the study of it, watching the errors of the players."[29]

Adams the autobiographer remains aloof and ironic as he watches himself watching the mistakes of others, crediting them with few successes, and reluctant, either as the narrator or the subject, to admit the value of his own achievements. The third-person narration enhances the detachment, and the past tense, without any sense of an ongoing later present, establishes an irrecoverable, disjunctive distance. The result is our impression not of a career, as in most autobiographies, still in process while being recorded, but

of a life already over and done with, a completed dramatic
script for a box-set behind a proscenium arch. Again and
again the tone suggests a long, closed history, seen in remote
perspective:

To his life as a whole he was a consenting, contracting party and partner
from the moment he was born to the moment he died. . . .

[The notion that Boston had solved the world's essential problems]
seemed to him the most curious social phenomenon he had to account
for in a long life. . . .

[Harvard undergraduates] were . . . the most formidable critics one
would care to meet, in a long life exposed to criticism. . . .

Many a shock was Henry Adams to meet in the course of a long
life. . . .

In a long experience, before and after, no one ever approached [the
brilliance of Swinburne's talk] . . .

The summer of the Spanish War began the Indian summer of life to
one who had reached sixty years of age, and cared only to reap in peace
such harvest as these sixty years had yielded.[30]

Watching the watcher, as if from beyond life, the narrator
concedes that the "identity" he is attempting to describe
and define is no more than "a bundle of disconnected memories."[31] Yet he is able to see in sharp enough outline the
figure he himself recalls—or half-remembers and half-in-
vents. (For he is not quite sure of the status of his impressions. Of an early train trip he writes: "This was the journey
he remembered. The actual journey may have been quite
different, but the actual journey has no interest for edu-

cation. The memory was all that mattered."³²) The Henry
Adams presented in the narrative has become a sort of "manikin" (the image clearly borrowed from *Sartor Resartus*), draped
in the costumes that are his successive "educations," and,
if a manikin may be animated sufficiently to act several
parts, he is assigned his successive roles: the private secretary, the dilettante, the editor, the professor, the speculative philosopher who likes to consider himself "the Virgin's
pilgrim." Only in this last role does an individual rather
than a type emerge, the character of a man born a century
too late, alienated in the modern "multiverse," obsessed
with a vision of vertiginous acceleration as his own spent
life slows to a complete stop.

Yet the finished chronicle is by no means as dreary as
the fixed expression on the manikin's face. *The Education of
Henry Adams*, which remains, I should think, the most impressive of American autobiographies, rises repeatedly above
its declared negations. Its power lies not only in the precision and color of its prose but also in the very devices that
reduce its protagonist: the imposition of a shaped confining
pattern, the attention to a range of external things, the skill
in capturing the ambiance of great cities and cultures, the
sophisticated satiric commentary, the portraits of memorable people—Lincoln and General Grant, Swinburne and
Thackeray, Gladstone and Earl Russell—the sharp reactions of a gifted ironic witness, who seeks no reflected glory
in eminent acquaintance. The record, to be sure, includes
some mistakes and contradictions; the narrator chides Harvard College in the 1850s for ignoring Karl Marx's *Capital*,
the first volume of which was actually not published even
in German till near the end of the following decade; and
he claims in one breath that no "education" could equal the
Embassy life in London, and in another that "the private

secretary" gained no real "education" at all in England. But factual consistency here matters less than the larger truths of fiction, and overstatement helps neutralize too frequent confessions of defeat. Key scenes, such as the meeting with Clarence King in Estes Park or the splendid dinner given by Monckton Milnes at Fryston, are prepared and presented with the care and calculation of an accomplished novelist. The most moving episode of all, Henry Adams's visit to his sister Louisa, stricken in Italy with fatal tetanus, is elaborately set against the soft sensuous beauty of the Appenines in mid-summer. And the epiphany which reveals the dynamo as a "symbol of infinity" and a portent of the frightening speed of the new century is timed deliberately as the climactic moment of a progress through the Gallery of Machines at the Paris exposition of 1900. From the beginning the narrator is aware of the ironies, comic or cruel, as in a Hardy novel, that may mock the protagonist's impressions or aspirations. But in the end, the last sentence of *The Education*, the ironist can scarcely suspect an even greater irony in his suggestion that, were Henry Adams able to return to earth on his hundredth birthday, he might possibly find at last "a world that sensitive and timid natures could regard without a shudder." Henry Adams's centenary year was 1938.

As readers of *The Education*, however, we ought not to be swayed unduly by a misjudgment reaching far beyond the closed design created by Adams's expressive style. As in the autobiographies of Wilde, Moore, and Gosse, we must accept the author's need of a controlling fiction and even a considerable degree of "theatricality," if we are to approach an understanding of the temperament he seeks both to mask and to reveal. Though the method of each of these in presenting specific scenes is highly circumstantial, to none of them do the precise details of a vocation or mental history matter as they did, say, to Newman or to Mill. All four are centrally concerned with the elusive identity of the self and the parts it has played. In the work of each we see autobiography moving toward one of its most characteristic twentieth-century forms, the autobiographical novel.

A Portrait of the Artist as a Young Man, to cite only the most distinguished example of that modern genre, presents a hero drawn closely from its author's own experience and in certain attitudes not unlike the disaffected aesthetes or intellectuals we have met in the self-histories of Wilde, Moore, Gosse, and Adams. Though Joyce knew nothing of *The Education,* his *Portrait* apparently owes something to the legend of Wilde's personality, if not to the abridged text of *De Profundis,* and it may be more specifically indebted to Moore and Gosse. Moore, at any rate, claimed to have done "the same thing, but much better, in *The Confessions of a Young Man.*"[33] The claim does not, of course, require our serious consideration, but we should note one signal advantage of Joyce over Moore and the others. Joyce presents himself as the novelist rather than the autobiographer, and as such, no matter how subjective the materials he chooses to exploit, he must create an independent protagonist, whose role we as readers will appraise quite apart from any question of the author's "theatricality" or any right to demand a true reflection of his real life and character.

❦ VI ❧

AUTOBIOGRAPHICAL FICTION

Miss Prism:	Memory, my dear Cecily, is the diary we all carry about with us.
Cecily:	Yes, but it usually chronicles the things that never happened, and couldn't possibly have happened. I believe that Memory is responsible for nearly all the three-volume novels that Mudie sends us.

—Oscar Wilde

In our lives we are always weaving novels.

—Anthony Trollope

Reviewing *Northanger Abbey* and *Persuasion* in 1821, Richard Whately commended the late Jane Austen for her choice of third-person narration as the best means of giving independent life to her characters. To be sure, he added, a few novelists had succeeded with story-telling in the *first* person. Daniel Defoe, in particular, was able to present the thoughts of an imaginary narrator "just as a real autobiographer might do," with the result that his books were "oftener mistaken for true narratives, than any fictions that were ever composed." In general, however, the first-person method, as practiced by Defoe, failed to please Whately since the narrator, who would also be the hero, risked a mistaken view of himself and "an offensive appearance of egotism."[1]

114

Nevertheless, despite such misgivings, the first-person novel persisted into the later nineteenth century when Jane Austen's elegant detachment was scarcely the literary mode. Sometimes the narrators in Victorian fiction are minor characters like Mr. Lockwood and Nelly Dean in *Wuthering Heights*. But often they are the protagonists, very much aware of the ego and the perils of egotism and even of the burden of a kind of self-creation through the act of writing— as in *Jane Eyre, David Copperfield, Great Expectations,* and *Harry Richmond*. Each of these four stories is presented as the "autobiography" of the narrator—indeed *Jane Eyre* specifically bears that subtitle. Each, following the conventions of the Bildungsroman, reflects something of the real author's own experience, not just Jane's autobiography or David's, Pip's, or Harry's, but in some measure Charlotte Brontë's, Dickens's, or George Meredith's. Each remains recognizably a novel, and none of these four, at any rate, is likely to be construed as the work of "a real autobiographer." Yet the fictional genre is no longer quite so distinct as it seemed in *Persuasion*, and it becomes less so among the later Victorians like George Gissing and Samuel Butler. As the twentieth century approaches, it proves increasingly difficult to distinguish between the autobiography invaded by fiction and the first-person fiction involving the autobiography of the author.

In an essay on the style of autobiography Jean Starobinski comments on "the ease with which a narrator may slip into fiction, a hazard that we ourselves are surely aware of from our own experience in recounting past events."[2] One of the most engaging of contemporary autobiographies illustrates—with no fear of inadvertent "slipping"—the closeness of the nonfictional form to fictional narrative. In *A Cab at the Door* V. S. Pritchett draws freely on the devices he has mastered as a writer of short stories. He sets up the scene with revealing detail and clear color, an eye for comic incident, and an understanding of class consciousness. He introduces much dialogue—far more than could be exactly recalled without the aid of precise notes or tape-recordings. The characters he remembers have preposterous Dickensian names, like Uncle Bugg and Aunt Lax, and they behave with fictional idiosyncrasy. His father, who dominates a household constantly on the move, resembles both Mr. Micawber and H. G. Wells's Teddy Ponderevo, but achieves, at least in these pages, his own vivid, larger-than-life identity. The narrator himself has no need or wish to be "theatrical" like Wilde or Moore; he is quietly detached, ironic, amused by his family circle, absorbed in his independent reading, and fascinated by his quickening powers of observation. Though he would greatly have preferred further schooling to apprenticeship in the leather trade, he brings a saving vision to his drudgery, a response to the human tragicomedy: "Story after story walked into the warehouse."[3] Eventually he is free to shape such stories into satisfying tidy patterns. The end of his memoir shows him recovered from a serious illness, setting off for Paris like Stephen Dedalus, but with none of Stephen's hubris.[4]

Nevertheless, though in its own way a demonstration of the novelist's art, A Cab at the Door reads as the work of "a real autobiographer," not as a fiction, for there is no apparent artifice set up between the author and the narrator. We assume instead a likely relationship to an actual life-history known to us from other sources, which offer an extrinsic validation both of the speaker's voice and the "reality" of the episodes he has chosen to re-create. Here, and perhaps to some extent in all autobiography, we knowingly accept some fictional distortion as a necessary adjunct to the teller's style, just as in any lively conversation we expect and indeed welcome the wit or sentiment or transparent hyperbole that may heighten a true personal report.

But if we conclude that all autobiography is to some degree fictional, we may question the reverse proposition. Thomas Wolfe's contention that "all serious work in fiction is autobiographical"[5] may seem little more than a rationalization of his own self-absorbed practice as a novelist. Anthony Powell, however, whose art is less egregiously subjective, makes a similar claim: "I have a theory that all novels are autobiographical," insofar as each is "the daydream of the writer."[6] Powell's own fiction, his *Dance to the Music of Time*, is no prolonged exercise in self-indulgence or self-revelation, but rather an extended review of his responses to the public years of his life. The serious novel, of course, may be much less obviously autobiographical even than that. *Vanity Fair, Our Mutual Friend, The Ambassadors, The Old Wives' Tale, The Rainbow*—none of these is intended to mirror the novelist's career, though each in its manner, choice of subject matter, emphasis, and imagery reveals much that may be characteristic of his temperament and vision. Nonetheless, avoiding broad generalizations about the novel and restricting our definition of autobiography to conscious self-revelation, we may still consider a large body of fiction designed, at least in part, to accomplish the central purposes of a "true" personal narrative.

Among late Victorians George Gissing provides a striking example of the operation, both direct and indirect, of the subjective impulse. Unlike the clinical French naturalists to whom he is often compared, Gissing experienced an urgent need, despite an apparent reticence and a real aloofness, to achieve some sort of personal justification. His late *Private Papers of Henry Ryecroft* imitates a form of direct first-person autobiography. Ryecroft, living in a simple country retirement, defensively reflects on his career, his choices and prejudices, his struggles as a young author against poverty and neglect, and his present self-approved retreat from a hostile society. His self-portrait in its essential details could readily serve as Gissing's own. Ryecroft's memories of his London life recall the precise misadventures that Gissing described in his early stories and that his biographers have amply documented, and Ryecroft's sentiments and trenchant judgments often draw with little or no change on entries in Gissing's own commonplace book. Gissing, however, strenuously objected when a reviewer, suspecting autobiography, equated his life and temperament with Ryecroft's. And there were indeed differences between the imagined character long since grown mellow in his misanthropy and the novelist who could neither enjoy nor transcend his estrangement.[7]

We see more of the actual Gissing, we may suppose, in the indirectly autobiographical novel, *New Grub Street*, which imposes a third-person perspective on a tortured self-scrutiny. The hero, defeated by the new journalism, is the long-suffering Edwin Reardon, clearly the author's surrogate and exact contemporary, drawn with intimate understanding and an unconcealed compassion. But Reardon is also seen, as Ryecroft is not, from a distance, the victim not just of circumstance but also of his own perverse will, betrayed by what is false within, and his portrait restrains Gissing's self-justification with a saving self-criticism. Besides, the biographical component is deployed among several more objective characters: Harold Biffen the "realist" eking out a bare livelihood by tutoring, the comical Mr. Whelpdale remembering a sad hungry experience in America, the querulous Alfred Yule thwarted in his scholarly ambition and bound to a wife wholly lacking his intellectual concerns. Gissing excelled neither in direct self-revelation nor in the invention of a fictional world beyond his immediate experience. In *New Grub Street*, surely his finest achievement, he found a middle course, a way of satisfying his personal need for confession and at the same time placing it at several removes from the literal fact and so shielding himself both from undue self-pity and from public misjudgment.

An effort like Gissing's to cloak self-appraisal or apology in the protective covering of fiction recurs in other late Victorian novelists and becomes common practice in the twentieth century. As in *New Grub Street* the autobiographical content is frequently diffused. In *Marius the Epicurean*, for example, Walter Pater assigns his gentle philosophic temper to Marius and his fiercer aestheticism to the rebellious Flavian. In *The Way of All Flesh* Samuel Butler presents a narrator, Mr. Overton, very like himself in disposition, prepared at every turn to express a gleeful Butlerian iconoclasm, but devised primarily to describe the career of Ernest Pontifex, which often nearly replicates that of the young Samuel Butler. Similarly in *Lord Jim* Marlow, a mature loquacious Joseph Conrad, seeks to fathom the enigma of the Conradian Jim, who is "one of us" yet perpetually elusive and alone. Henry Green amusingly reported how he liked "to bring others in when I wrote about myself in order to blame as much as possible on others."[8] And Patrick White more recently has explained with due gravity the personal sanctions of his art:

Sexual ambivalence helped drive me in on myself. Lacking flamboyance, cursed with reserve, I chose fiction, or more likely it was chosen for me, as the means of introducing to a disbelieving audience the cast of contradictory characters of which I am composed.[9]

If the principal English and American autobiographers, not excluding De Quincey, are characteristically too reticent to admit any considerable degree of really intimate confession, the autobiographical novelists are free to explore their personal traumas, sexual fantasies, and moral nonconformities without embarrassment or fear of being directly identified with the experience described. While the modern autobiographer self-consciously avoids self-analysis lest he expose his inner life to a reductive psychology, the post-Freudian novelist psychologizes with no such compunction. But even nineteenth-century writers, innocently ignorant of dark complexes, were reluctant to divulge idiosyncrasies of thought or conduct which seemed unique, unorthodox, or actually antisocial. Mill, whose essay *On Liberty* vigorously defends eccentricity, strove in his *Autobiography* to present his responses to his unusual education as normal, rational, and representative. The colorful cast of Victorian eccentrics appears mostly in the novels rather than in the "true" personal histories, but many of their quirks and quiddities derive from the odd predilections of the novelists.

Though many Victorians "thrilled," as George Eliot did, to Rousseau's apparently unabashed self-revelation, the *Confessions* had but limited acknowledged impact on formal Victorian autobiography.[10] Yet it may well have been in the mind of the foremost Victorian novelist as he began the central work of his career. The second paragraph of Rousseau's preface ends with a teasing defiance: "Whether Nature did wisely in breaking the mould with which she formed me, is a question which can only be determined after having read these books." Dickens begins *David Copperfield*, one of the trial titles of which was *The Copperfield Confessions*, with a more modest challenge to the reader: "Whether I shall turn out to be the hero of my own life, or whether that station will be held by someone else, these pages must show." The similarities between the two openings seem to me more than merely coincidental.

David Copperfield is the first of Dickens's novels to be written in the first person and as such an experiment affording new opportunities for self-analysis, reflection, and reverie. As John Forster first revealed, the fiction had its origin in an actual autobiographical fragment, a painful "confession" Dickens was unable to complete, recounting his servitude at Warren's blacking factory, which he transcribed with little change in the chapter concerned with David's misery in the wine warehouse of Murdstone and Grinby. Other sections of the novel also have a firm basis in remembered experience—notably the courtship of Dora, which recalls the infatuation with Maria Beadnell. Dickens obviously had a strong personal stake in the narrative, and some years after its publication he acknowledged its attraction: "I never can approach the book with perfect composure (it had such perfect possession of me when I wrote it)."[11] In writing, he must often have identified with David, but he may also have been attempting self-appraisal in the drawing of other characters quite unlike David: the aggressive Steerforth, with his Byronic restlessness and all his dangerous mesmeric charm; the invincible Micawber, verbally transcending all vicissitudes; even, some readers now argue, the compulsively scribbling, gently mad Mr. Dick. Yet the observation of the real and the tangible in setting and the great power of invention completely subsume any personal source or merely subjective impulse. The novel calls into being a Dickensian world with an autonomous life of its own, with energy, exuberance, and primary colors and little or no final dependence on the secret history of Charles Dickens.

David Copperfield, after all, must be understood as David's autobiography and not as Dickens's. David eventually achieves his own distinct identity, but less by self-centered introspection than by noting with the novelist's sharp eye the conduct of those about him. His own need for direction and serious commitment is made clear to him by the bad and good examples of friends and relations who have either succumbed to wayward passions or with a struggle managed to resist them: Clara Copperfield, Em'ly, Steerforth, Rosa Dartle, Annie Strong, Aunt Betsy. Each of these provides a variation on his central theme, repeatedly announced as the conquest of "my undisciplined heart."[12] The deepest subjectivity lies in his fascination with the functioning of memory, the resurgence and reenactment of the past. David more than recollects the scene of Annie Strong's declaration of fidelity: "I see and hear, rather than remember, as I write about it." And he relives the Yarmouth tempest in all its fury: "I do not recall but see it done; for it happens again before me." He is concerned, of course, with "my own heart . . . in its secret experience" and the menace of a "distempered fancy," but like Wordsworth he is eager to relate his hopes and fears and unforgotten past to a general psychology, a sense of the "ordinary." He presents the mysterious sensation of *déjà vu* as "the strong feeling to which, perhaps, no one is quite a stranger," and, again, as "a feeling that comes over us occasionally" and that all of us know. Throughout his narrative he would have us believe that his remarkable gift of recall is always within the higher range of normalcy, differing, if at all, from the common in degree but not in kind. By the end we should have little doubt that David actually is the hero of his own life or that his heroism, like that of Dickens, lies less in the projection of a powerful ego than in the strength of the sympathetic imagination that animates and objectifies his story.

Among Victorian novels *The Mill on the Floss* stands closest to *David Copperfield* in the vivid depiction of childhood, and the initial impulse behind its composition was similarly "confessional." Though George Eliot credited Rousseau with

first awakening her to "deep reflection," her own most personal probing of the psyche was to be a safely detached
third-person fiction rather than a direct autobiography. As
a child Maggie Tulliver the protagonist greatly resembles
in spirit, temper, and intelligence the young Mary Ann
Evans whom we know from other records. George Eliot
presents the thought and action of this alter ego from a
distance, with sympathy, amusement, and quiet irony. And
she is hardly less successful in the portrayal of Tom Tulliver, who is the image of Mary Ann's brother Isaac. But
when eventually she turns to describe the spiritual conflicts
of the adolescent Maggie and her unhappy alienation from
Tom, who is now the censorious, unforgiving Isaac, her
narrative becomes unfortunately engaged and defensive. The
heroine now is "poor Maggie," whose "young heart" in all
its high aspiration is cruelly misunderstood by a narrow-
minded provincial middle class. Though Maggie's final tragic
fate was planned from the outset, the ending of the novel
seems fortuitous, too deliberately contrived, and marred by
sentimentality. The estrangement of brother and sister, un-
resolved in real life, must here be resolved in a melodramatic
death. Maggie in effect is punished by a parochial code
which George Eliot rejected, though never wholly escaped.
Henry James wished that Maggie had eloped with Stephen
Guest. We might have preferred to see her run off alone—
to London and to George Eliot's strenuous career in literature. As it is, she must somehow atone for the novelist's
half-suppressed sense of guilt in having repudiated the conventions and proprieties of her own inheritance. If the first
half of *The Mill on the Floss* gains much in intimacy from
recollected personal detail, the second part, though often
cogent in social analysis, suffers distortion from the effort
to satisfy an unforgotten private need.

The most striking examples of a similar subjectivity in

early-modern fiction, Lawrence's *Sons and Lovers* and Joyce's
Portrait, again illustrate both the strength and possible
weakness of the autobiographical mode. We can readily and
reasonably identify Paul Morel with the young Lawrence
by reference to the latter's poems and letters, the copious
reminiscences of his family and friends, and even published
interviews with his neighbors. We can verify descriptions
of setting by comparison with actual photographs; the Bestwood of the novel is clearly the Eastwood near Nottingham,
and the "Morel" houses have become literary shrines. Above
all, we have Lawrence's confession, commenting on Paul's
instability, that "one sheds one's sicknesses in books—re-
peats and presents again one's emotions, to be master of
them."[13]

We can also establish the relation at nearly every point
of Stephen Dedalus's development to that of Joyce, the
Dublin of his childhood, the Jesuit education, the rebellion
against the family, and the final exile from Ireland. As with
Lawrence, we have ample documentation: correspondence,
a most substantial biography, memoirs by the originals of
characters in the novel. Besides, we have warrant from
Joyce's letter to his Spanish translator to interpret the title
as self-reflexive. *A Portrait of the Artist as a Young Man*, Joyce
explained, derives from labels on self-portraits by the old
masters in a picture gallery.[14] Joyce, of course, expected us
to understand "*the* artist" as typical, no less than individual.
All the same, we may be reminded of Rembrandt's self-
portraits at which we look not just as pictures but also as
revealing images of the artist himself.

Awareness of such extrinsic data makes it difficult to
judge Lawrence's novel or Joyce's in purely aesthetic terms,
without reference to the author's life and character or to
facts he withheld that might have elucidated obscurities in

the text. Neither book is as variegated and inventive as *David Copperfield*, as independent of materials outside the fiction. Rather the imagination in each, though operating at a high level, serves not so much to create, as to re-create, an intense personal experience and ultimately to relate every significant detail of the action to the subjective life of a hero who is close to the author as the author once was or as he now chooses to remember himself. In each a good measure of primary substance resembles that of *The Prelude*, drawn, that is, from keenly recollected impressions, moments of insight or spots of time, Joyce's "epiphanies" or Lawrence's flashes of the flame of life, symbols of individual or isolated identity. The virtue of the subjective approach in each is that it may render the sensation or emotion with sudden fresh immediacy. The limitation is that the fiction, like many autobiographies, may become a mere shedding of private sickness or an intricate exercise in self-justification.

Sons and Lovers begins as a family novel with a number of sharply delineated characters and a beautifully realized social setting, one of the finest achievements of British realism. It ends as distinctly Paul Morel's story, an exploration of his troubled psyche, at times approaching the abstraction of a reductive case history. Paul is now quite alone, self-centered but lacking his father's ardent selfhood, probing his mixed emotions, proud but miserably unhappy, ready to impute his own failure at love to the tremulous Miriam. His problem in clinical terms (which Lawrence fortunately did not know until most of the novel was complete) is all too obviously a mother-fixation or Oedipus complex, and it persists relentlessly after his mother's death. Though quite conscious of the malady, Lawrence as narrator seems to endorse Paul's attitudes and personal "religion" and to rationalize his neurotic self-absorption. The last chapter,

"Derelict," however, prepares us to leave Paul broken, disconsolate, and even suicidal. Then unaccountably the very last paragraph intimates his survival in some purposeful future that the novel itself nowhere prefigures:

But no, he would not give in. Turning sharply, he walked towards the city's gold phosphorescence. His fists were shut, his mouth set fast. He would not take that direction, to the darkness to follow her. He walked towards the faintly humming, glowing town, quickly.

Lawrence himself, of course, did survive as the modern artist and the lonely nomadic prophet. But in ending *Sons and Lovers* on a positive note, however true he may be to his own subsequent experience, he is less than faithful to the image of himself that he has projected in Paul Morel. The real epilogue to the autobiographical content of the novel may well be the short sketch written years later, "Return to Bestwood" (significantly, the place retains its fictional name), in which Lawrence, now speaking in his own person but still as dogmatic as Paul, argues gently with his dead mother and firmly defends his repudiation of her values.[15]

Joyce's *Portrait* likewise invites the reader to look before and after, beyond the text, for clues to interpretation. But the text itself has a tighter unity than *Sons and Lovers*, and the protagonist has a more ambiguous relation to the author. We are able to empathize readily with Stephen the small child and the schoolboy, and to assume that the narrator considers him with similar indulgence. As we continue, however, we find the sympathy with which Stephen the "young man" is drawn frequently qualified and undercut by irony of a kind totally missing in Lawrence's novel. Eventually we must determine how much of the *Portrait* is intentionally satiric and in what light we are to assess Stephen's endowment, revolt, and ambition. The dates appended to the last page, 1904–1914, establish the distance from which the author, constantly revising his narrative, viewed in detachment a boyhood and adolescence in all essentials like his own. Unless we are impressed, as some readers are, by Stephen's one creative effort, the sentimental *fin-de-siècle* villanelle of "enchanted days," we must conclude that the "young man" is not yet an artist or even that he will hardly achieve that status in his maturity. Still we cannot be sure what Joyce would have us think of the poem, though we may note that it compares favorably enough with most of the pieces he saved for publication in *Chamber Music*. We are surely expected to see an irony, of which Stephen is not conscious, in his late diary: "Mother is putting my new secondhand clothes in order"—as if the rebel were a child being abetted in his childish plan to run away from home. And we may decide that the bravado with which that same entry concludes is to be properly regarded as excessive overstatement: "Welcome, O life! I go to encounter for the millionth time the reality of experience and to forge in the smithy of my soul the uncreated conscience of my race." But we hesitate to judge the boast when we discover that Joyce himself expressed an almost identical sentiment, with no trace of irony or self-mockery, in a letter to his wife, written before he had published a single volume of his fiction: "I am one of the writers of this generation who are perhaps creating at last a conscience in the soul of this wretched race."[16]

Joyce, to be sure, far more than Stephen earned the right to make such a claim. But we have too much evidence of Joyce's egomania throughout his life to be certain that he would wholly condemn Stephen's overweening aesthetic pride and self-satisfaction or even his messianic delusions. Our familiarity with the larger Joyce canon, all in effect one vast, intricate, correlated self-expression, draws us outside the *Portrait* to its origins, parallels, and sequel. The evolution of the novel may be traced from a short autobiographical sketch of 1904 entitled "A Portrait of the Artist," through the long fragment called *Stephen Hero*, to the cunning artifice of the final 1916 text. We may then, if we will, move on to *Ulysses*, where Stephen, returning from exile, is sadly reduced in stature and pretension, and even to *Finnegans Wake*, where "Shem or James," according to one explicator, is "another Stephen, egocentric and literary, author of *Ulysses* and Joyce's other works."[17] Taken all together, these extrinsic materials complicate our view of Stephen both as an invented character and as a partial image of the young Joyce.

As autobiographical novels both *Sons and Lovers* and the *Portrait*, whether engaged or defensively ironic, may be read as apologias, testaments of defiance and dedication. If so, both leave something to be desired, insofar as the reader may fail to develop any great affection for either Paul or Stephen or even any sense that either hero ultimately has sufficient vision beyond the self to attain the perspective of the heroic artist. Yet the value of each book is larger than its original subjective bearings. Each as a work of fiction is presented by a third-person narrator more vibrant than his surrogate, a Lawrence more resilient than Paul, a Joyce more creative than Stephen. *Sons and Lovers* captures with a selfless power the tensions of family life and the reality of a whole group of characters who live quite apart from Lawrence's declared will to shed his sickness in the narrative. And *A Portrait* by subtle contrivance of image and symbol and virtuosity of language achieves the harmony and design of an art about which Stephen the aesthete can only speculate.

Though Lawrence and Joyce attacked each other for eccentric and self-regarding views of life and literature, both, especially in the major work of their middle years, attempted to move "beyond egotism" towards a general psychology and a broadened acceptance of fallible human beings.[18] Autobiographical fiction, however, sometimes more narrowly focused than theirs, persisted among their contemporaries. Women writers in particular, usually distrustful of nonfictional self-scrutiny, found the subjective novel a congenial medium. Dorothy Richardson, for example, indebted in part to Joyce's techniques, followed through the many volumes of her *Pilgrimage* the stream of consciousness of Miriam Henderson, whose impressions, nonadventures, hopes, and fears apparently at almost every moment paralleled her own. May Sinclair, like Lawrence, probed a child's relationship to a too possessive parent, and the child, whether a daughter as in *Mary Olivier* or a son as in *Arnold Waterlow*, reflects all too starkly the experience and sensibility of the author. Meanwhile, Virginia Woolf was developing a far firmer command of form, strong enough to re-order her own mixed memories. In *To the Lighthouse*, her personal masterpiece, she achieved both intimacy and distance: Mr. and Mrs. Ramsey translate her intensely remembered father and mother to another time and setting, and Lily Briscoe, observing the family circle from the outside, represents the detached artist who was her creator.

Many later novelists have recognized the challenge of subjective intrusion, and a few have seen the threat of solipsism and narcissism. Henry Miller had no qualms about giving himself free entree to his *Tropic of Cancer:* "I have," he declared, "painstakingly indicated throughout the book that the hero is myself. I don't use 'heroes,' incidentally, nor do I write novels. I am the hero, and the book is myself."[19] More recently, on the other hand, the late John Gardner, whose narratives are studiously objective, remarked that "keeping personal ego out of one's art is one of the hardest things about writing fiction."[20] Other contemporary writers, differing widely from each other in style and content—Christopher Isherwood, William Golding, Samuel Beckett, Doris Lessing, Saul Bellow, John Barth, and many more—draw frequently on private experience, sometimes to the enrichment of their analysis, often to the circumscribing of the range of their invention. Some of these present not so much an emotional development, or even a sensibility in which the sympathetic reader may share, as their own struggles with a fictional craft of increasingly private meanings. Their novels then may become involuted narratives of the effort of the protagonist, himself a novelist, to write an autobiographical novel much like that in which he appears.[21] *David Copperfield* achieved that end with conspicuous success, but David's art as narrator lay in his ability to evoke dramatic scenes and characters and not in any need to discuss the problems of evocation. A more self-conscious fiction locked in upon itself can scarcely be expected to attain a comparable energy or resonance.

❧ VII ❧

POETRY AND THE PRINCIPLE
OF SELF

Poetry, and the principle of Self, . . . are the God
and Mammon of the world.

—Shelley

Ce que on dit de soi est toujours poésie.

—Ernest Renan

PUBLISHED within a few weeks of each other in 1850,
the two major long autobiographical poems of the English
nineteenth century, *In Memoriam* and *The Prelude*, differ
greatly in tone and texture, yet share a common problem
in the definition of the speaker or narrator. Tennyson, re-
senting a too personal reading of his elegy, claimed that the
"I" was "not always the poet speaking of himself, but the
voice of the human race speaking thro' [him]."[1] Wordsworth
during some forty years of intermittent work on *The Prelude*
apparently had no disposition to suggest that the "I" of the
poem should be construed as other than the true voice of
William Wordsworth. Nevertheless, he assumed, as we have
seen, that the psychological experience he was describing
was broadly representative, or at least rooted in the circumstances of "ordinary" life, and so available in some measure
to other sensitive souls. Like Tennyson, he therefore moved
freely from the particular to the general, from a private first
person singular to mankind's first person plural.

In even the most personal poetry the self of a poet, insofar as he submits to the discipline and distance of meter, figurative language, and often stanzaic form, is perpetually more elusive and ambiguous than the self of the narrator of a subjective prose fiction. A mid-Victorian essay attempting to define autobiography, posited that the genre demanded "always the voice of a living man which speaks to us of himself" and then went on to contend that

the poet is always to some extent an autobiographer. Speaking the language which takes its form and sequence from his own emotions, he must often record these as his own.[2]

But to say this is to ignore the fact that the "I," like Tennyson's frequently, may be suprapersonal or, if indeed individual, spoken through a more or less dramatic mask.

Byron, for example, almost from the beginning, on the evidence especially of *Childe Harold*, was accused of a hypertrophy of the ego, and indeed Byron the man may often have exhibited an egregious pride, conceit, and self-will. But the titanic voice of Harold, as he aligns himself with elemental powers, is a deliberate invention rather than a simple echo of the poet; it is the expressive cry of a literary construct, the "Byronic hero." The real Byron, though with still other masks, is, we may suppose, to be found, if anywhere, in the poet's incomparable letters and in the infinitely varied digressions of *Don Juan*. In his preface to the latter Byron mocks Wordsworth's declaration that the narrator of "The Thorn" is not the poet but a garrulous retired sea-captain. Well, then, he tells us, the adventures of his Don Juan are to be recounted "by a Spanish Gentleman in a village in the Sierra Morena on the road between Monasterio and Seville, sitting at the door of a Posada, with the

Curate of the hamlet on his right hand, a Segar in his mouth, a jug of Malaga or perhaps 'right Sherris' before him on a small table containing the relics of an Olla Podrida."[3] The actual narrator, of course, is no such distinct or limited a personage. If he is not precisely Byron, he is a worldly-wise observer, satiric, racy, tender, robust, reminiscential, speaking a fluent colloquial English, charged with the energy, wit, and sentiment we assume to have been Byron's own. Yet we must judge his vitality in the context of the poem and not simply as a reflection of the more genial aspects of the protean poet.

Shelley's apparent subjectivity is likewise equivocal. His early "Alastor," replete as it is with symbols of self-consciousness, mirroring pools, subterranean caves, the yellow flowers of the narcissus, is the allegory of a poet isolated by his own sensibility, defeated by "the spirit of solitude" within. Though the poet-hero has obvious Shelleyan attributes, the poem is less a self-portrait than a reminder of the perils threatening a typical Romantic artist. Some of Shelley's lyrics—the several pieces "To Jane," for instance—may be read without loss as statements of personal feeling, the sheer music of which invites our participation. But a much greater poem, the memorable "Ode to the West Wind," suffers from the intrusion of what seems little more than a maudlin self-pity: "I fall upon the thorns of life! I bleed!" The artifices of the pastoral convention invoked in "Adonais" partially conceal a similar agony of self-contemplation; among those lamenting the death of Adonais comes one readily identifiable as Shelley himself,

> one frail Form,
> A phantom among men; companionless
> As the last cloud of an expiring storm

> Whose thunder is its knell; he, as I guess,
> Had gazed on Nature's naked loveliness,
> Actaeon-like, and now he fled astray
> With feeble steps o'er the world's wilderness,
> And his own thoughts, along that rugged way,
> Pursued, like raging hounds, their father and their prey.
>
> A pardlike Spirit beautiful and swift—
> A Love in desolation masked;—a Power
> Girt round with weakness. . . .

But whether or not this passage strikes a false note, it jars but little in the rich orchestration of an otherwise generally selfless tribute. Shelley's most sustained poetic autobiography is the triumphant "Epipsychidion," full of private fantasies and symbols, yet lifted by the power of sound and structure into a unique, impersonal celebration of erotic love. In "A Defence of Poetry," his true personal apologia, Shelley sets up the basic conflict between poetry and the principle of self, between the life of the imagination and a self-seeking materialism. By "the principle of self" he wished to connote the self-interest of an acquisitive society, but he must also have had in mind the self-regard that threatened to encroach upon his own broad sympathies as upon the vision of every dedicated Romantic poet.

Disturbed by the record of Shelley's irregular conduct, Matthew Arnold was prepared to read the man into the poetry:

Let no one suppose that a want of humour and a self-delusion such as Shelley's have no effect upon a man's poetry. The man Shelley, in very truth, is not entirely sane, and Shelley's poetry is not entirely sane either. The Shelley of actual life is a vision of beauty and radiance, indeed, but availing nothing, effecting nothing. And in poetry, no less than in life, he is "a beautiful *and ineffectual* angel, beating in the void his luminous wings in vain."[4]

So concludes one of Arnold's last essays, an impatient review of Edward Dowden's biography. His view of Shelley, however, was fixed many years earlier when he diagnosed the failure of the "moderns" as a willful subjectivity, an effort, particularly conspicuous in Shelley and Keats, to achieve self-expression at the expense of carefully delineated action. Shelley's "incurable want . . . of a sound subject matter" was simply, he thought, the common malady of a self-conscious introspective modern literature, a weakness unfortunately being encouraged rather than corrected by the taste of the time. In the 1853 preface to his own poems he scorned a "modern critic" who had remarked that "a true allegory of the state of one's own mind" was "perhaps the highest thing that one can attempt in the way of poetry." "The highest problem," Arnold retorted, "of an art which imitates actions! No assuredly, it is not, it can never be so: no great poetical work ever has been produced with such an aim."[5]

Arnold prepared the 1853 preface to explain his suppression of "Empedocles on Etna," the title piece of his second volume and the most ambitious of all his early poems. Though not exactly a true personal allegory, "Empedocles," despite its ancient setting, presents what Arnold recognized as "modern problems" in a typically modern form, a "dialogue of the mind with itself," the sort of irritable, unavailing self-colloquy that the young poet knew only too well from his own experience. "Sohrab and Rustum," however, which replaced "Empedocles" in the new volume, was less than a complete success as a convincing demonstration of the advantages of narrative action over dispirited introspection. For all its genuine pathos and consistency of texture, "Sohrab" remains too self-consciously Homeric, both in its noble characters and in its overuse of extended simile, too patently a contrived literary exercise. And more ironic than its many calculated ironies is the fact that a number of latterday readers, without much warrant, have given the objective story an ominously subjective significance as a clue to the poet's repressed resentment of his dominant father.[6] At any rate, Arnold's most memorable verse, from all phases of his career, is neither epical nor dramatic; it is lyric, often elegiac in tone, more personal than as critic he could have wished: "Dover Beach," "The Buried Life," several pieces in the Marguerite sequence. The truly representative poem of 1853 was not "Sohrab" but "The Scholar-Gipsy," a sort of modern pastoral, at once a warm nostalgic evocation of the Oxford countryside and an angry polemic against the "strange disease of modern life" that was blighting all direct response and steadiness of vision. And part of the indictment of the sick age was characteristically (for the literary critic in Arnold was never far behind the lyric poet) an attack on the sorry state of modern letters, which nourished a pervasive malaise and applauded a melancholy spokesman:

> amongst us one
> Who most has suffered, takes dejectedly
> His seat upon the intellectual throne;
> And all his store of sad experience he
> Lays bare of wretched days;
> Tells us his misery's birth and growth and signs,
> And how the dying spark of hope was fed,
> And how the breast was soothed, and how the head,
> And all his hourly varied anodynes.

Though Arnold was unwilling in later life to say so, the suffering author recounting his griefs was almost certainly the poet of *In Memoriam*.[7] The "intellectual throne," a phrase appropriated from "The Palace of Art," was surely meant as an ironic description of the post of Laureate that Tennyson recently had accepted, and the "hourly varied anodynes" must have been intended as a reference to the short lyrics of the elegy, which Tennyson's text itself compared to "dull narcotics soothing pain." But Arnold's condescending dismissal of both poet and poem simply reflected his distrust of the sad subjective impulse, which he was striving to repress in himself, rather than an understanding of Tennyson's private and public voices or a just estimate of the poem as a whole and the positive resolution to which it aspires.

In Memoriam actually anticipates any charge of subjectivity that might be brought against it.[8] A short pastoral dialogue near the beginning presents three travelers as they approach the shepherd-mourner. The first deplores what seems to him an excessive sentimentalism:

> "This fellow would make weakness weak
> And melt the waxen hearts of men."

The second cynically suspects self-advertisement:

> "Let him be,
> He loves to make parade of pain,
> That with his piping he may gain
> The praise that comes to constancy."

The third, ignoring the bucolic setting, speaks for a purposeful modern society, impatient with a self-indulgent retreat:

> "Is this the hour
> For private sorrow's barren song,

> When more and more the people throng
> The chairs and thrones of civil power?
>
> "A time to sicken and to swoon
>   When Science reaches forth her arms
>   To feel from world to world, and charms
> Her secret from the latest moon?"

But the poet has at the moment no will to celebrate the progress of either democracy or science. In a subsequent exchange between the muses, the stern epical Urania and the sensitive elegiac Melpomene, he still clearly supports the latter, who defends her concern with personal love and loss rather than with more august mysteries. He must renew his own sense of selfhood and wholeness, almost destroyed by the death of his friend, before he can begin to relate his life and poetry to any large objective context.

Deeply self-conscious and ambivalent in his lonely introspection, the poet wonders whether his memory has misrepresented the past as "pure and perfect" and, more frighteningly, whether his present misery has somehow deranged his personality:

> Or has the shock, so harshly given,
> Confused me like the unhappy bark
>
> That strikes by night a craggy shelf,
>   And staggers blindly ere she sink?
>   And stunned me from my power to think
> And all my knowledge of myself;
>
> And made me that delirious man
>   Whose fancy fuses old and new,
>   And flashes into false and true,
> And mingles all without a plan?

The loss of self-knowledge, the confusion of time-levels, the failure to distinguish false from true, subjective from objective realities—these are precisely the symptoms of what we now call schizophrenia. In our time, however, the condition has been extolled by R. D. Laing as a literary asset and deliberately cultivated by a number of disaffected contemporary poets. Unlike these, the poet of *In Memoriam* recognizes and resists the state and resolutely struggles to affirm his sanity and personal identity. "But what am I?" he asks at the depth of his self-questioning, when he is prepared only to answer helplessly,

> An infant crying in the night,
> An infant crying for the light,
> And with no language but a cry.

He chooses the image with care, punning on the root meaning of *infant*, "not yet speaking," without language, inarticulate. Elsewhere he has speculated on infancy as the first stage in the gradual emergence of a distinct selfhood:

> The baby new to earth and sky,
>   What time his tender palm is prest
>   Against the circle of the breast,
> Has never thought that "this is I:"
>
> But as he grows he gathers much,
>   And learns the use of "I" and "me,"
>   And finds "I am not what I see,
> And other than the things I touch."
>
> So rounds he to a separate mind
>   From whence clear memory may begin,
>   As through the frame that binds him in
> His isolation grows defined.

The poet's argument here foreshadows both Jacques Lacan's attention to "the primary alienation of the *infans* from 'himself' and the subsequent discovery of his Self," and also Erik Erikson's account of "the battle for autonomy" when the infant first learns to distinguish his "worlds as 'I' and 'you' and 'me' and 'mine.' "[9] But the importance of the passage lies in the poet's capacity for public speech, for generalization beyond the ego, rather than in any original contribution to identity psychology. As the poem continues, the speaker becomes increasingly aware of the need for an adult perspective on "the soul within" and the objective world without. He learns that his self-absorbed grief may have distorted his vision of ongoing life. He perceives the falsity of dreams and the psychic displacement they may bring; dreaming, he has found "a trouble" in his dead friend's eye, but now

> I wake, and I discern the truth;
> It is the trouble of my youth
> That foolish sleep transfers to thee.

In a later jargon the trouble of his youth is the "identity crisis" he must confront and overcome.

In Memoriam, nonetheless, remains a highly subjective poem. The resolution of the crisis demands a fitting adjustment between the subjective and the objective, between "faith" and "knowledge," rather than a repudiation of either one. Faith is not a matter of willful self-indulgence, for that produces only delusion and bewilderment. It is an act of disinterested intuition, a mystical, Tennysonian spot of time, the sort of ineffable illumination that flashes suddenly and briefly upon the poet as he reads his friend's letters on the quiet lawn at Somersby:

So word by word, and line by line,
   The dead man touched me from the past,
   And all at once it seemed at last
The living soul was flashed on mine,

And mine in this was wound, and whirled
   About empyreal heights of thought,
   And came on that which is, and caught
The deep pulsations of the world,

Aeonian music measuring out
   The steps of Time—the shocks of Chance—
   The blows of Death. At length my trance
Was cancelled, stricken through with doubt.

As this crucial revelation ends, the language drops abruptly from the eloquent to the anticlimactic ordinary, for the experience has effected a transformation of the self ultimately beyond description:

Vague words! but ah, how hard to frame
   In matter-moulded forms of speech
   Or even for intellect to reach
Through memory that which I became.

But the epiphany results in a strong new sanction for a subjective religious faith, independent of theological proofs and evidences, a reason of the heart, like Pascal's, beyond all reasoning:

If e'er when faith had fallen asleep,
   I heard a voice "believe no more"
   And heard an ever-breaking shore
That tumbled in the Godless deep;

> A warmth within the breast would melt
> The freezing reason's colder part,
> And like a man in wrath the heart
> Stood up and answered, "I have felt."

And it also provides a basis for faith in the value and continuity of a selfhood, strong though disciplined—as the last section before the epilogue insists, a "faith that comes of self-control."

Knowledge, on the other hand, looks outward: "For knowledge is of things we see," things we can "prove" by sense experience. To the poet of *In Memoriam*, as to most Victorians, science, the formidable new knowledge of the nineteenth century, is empirical, perceptual rather than conceptual. Having attained the balance of faith in an ordered universe, he can regard scientific observation and discovery as objective material data, no longer, as he feared in his early lyrics, inimical to the life of the spirit. And he can also accept the tools of a poetic knowledge, "the matter-moulded forms of speech," of which he senses his own mastery. His recovery is complete when he can recognize his calling and his responsibility for communication to a society beyond himself and all his "vacant yearning":

> I will not shut me from my kind,
> And, lest I stiffen into stone,
> I will not eat my heart alone,
> Nor feed with sighs a passing wind. . . .
>
> What find I in the highest place,
> But mine own phantom chanting hymns?
> And on the depths of death there swims
> The reflex of a human face.

He has achieved in effect his real identity—what the psychologist will call "ego integrity"—in work and fellowship.

At the close of the clegy he affirms his larger intuition of meaning, but also "the lesser faith / That sees the course of human things," the worth of history, and the utility of knowledge; with the simile drawn appropriately from his vocation as poet, he can see at last, or rather

>   see in part
>   That all, as in some piece of art,
>   Is toil cöoperant to an end.

Though many of the details of *In Memoriam* are too private to be wholly intelligible without reference to his biography, Tennyson wished the poem to be read as a representative account of "the way of the soul," told in the public first person. T. S. Eliot once called him "the saddest of all English poets, among the Great in Limbo."[10] Yet Tennyson was reluctant all his life to "make parade of pain," or indeed to show directly any other personal feelings. In dramatic monologues throughout his career he was able to mask, and so to distance, some of his deepest emotions by assigning them to remote correlatives, Mariana, Ulysses, Tithonus, Tiresias, the Ancient Sage, through all of whom he might speak sympathetically yet without obvious subjective commitment. As his fame grew, however, he found a public increasingly eager to approach his work (as if it were all a sort of literal confession), ever readier to pry into his personal affairs, and more and more flagrantly to encroach upon his actual privacy. On one occasion he is reported to have driven off with his walking-stick a flock of sheep that he nearsightedly mistook for yet another band of inquisitive Americans on pilgrimage to his home at Farringford. If he sought—and found—a large audience, he nonetheless refused to pander to "the many-headed beast" of popularity, and at times he looked enviously at such a poet as his brother Charles, who was willing to abandon publication altogether rather than suffer gossip and crude exploitation:

> And you have missed the irreverent doom
> Of those that wear the Poet's crown;
> Hereafter, neither knave nor clown
> Shall hold their orgies at your tomb.[11]

He himself feared the excesses of his own reputation; privately, in a notebook, he scored both his too intense admirers and those who would surely one day repudiate his achievement: "While I live, the owls! / When I die, the *ghouls*!!!"[12] If the former attempted to sophisticate his thought, the latter would seek to destroy the art that had affirmed his very identity.

Other Victorian poets, sharing the legacy of Romantic subjectivity, were as circumspect as Tennyson or Arnold in avoiding excessive self-revelation. The Pre-Raphaelites and Swinburne, despite distinctly personal signatures of style and content, resisted all efforts to equate the "I" of the poem with the life of the poet. Swinburne's lyric monologues, chants, and pagan hymns, submerging his own strange fantasies and aberrant visions beneath tidal waves of sound and surf, were designed both to destroy public complacency and to assert the autonomy of the art work. Even his poetic autobiography "Thalassius," celebrating, in the third person, the spiritual growth of a child of the sun and the sea, conceals in symbol and allegory the specifics of his intense, though largely vicarious, experience. Christina Rossetti, whose love songs and devotional pieces seem more direct, believed that a poem should be "a genuine lyric cry" but

at the same time an embodiment of universal feeling artic-
ulated by an individual poet.[13] She could hardly have imagined that exegetes of a later time would attempt to discover
in the narrative of "Goblin Market" a hidden confession of
a guilty amour thwarted at the last minute by the intervention of her pious sister Maria.[14] Dante Gabriel Rossetti,
who enshrined his memories and impressions of a rather
more various eroticism in the ornate, depersonalizing décor
of *The House of Life*, was distressed to the point of almost
complete collapse by the charge of unmanly "fleshiness"
that Robert Buchanan levelled against both his person and
his poetry. But his sonnets—discreet, abstract, metaphysical, concerned certainly with love but also with many other
human values—should themselves have been sufficient ref-
utation of a censorious philistinism. One among them, at
any rate, as profoundly personal as any, presents in unforgettable terms the burden of selfhood that every modern
man must carry; the poet is speculating on the "lost days"
of his life, the missed opportunities for action beyond the
self:

> I do not see them here; but after death
> God knows I know the faces I shall see,
> Each one a murdered self, with low last breath.
> "I am thyself,—what hast thou done to me?"
> "And I—and I—thyself," (lo! each one saith,)
> "And thou thyself to all eternity!"

Rossetti's sense of the inescapable self anticipates the mood
of Gerard Manley Hopkins in his last "terrible sonnets."
From the time of his first major poem the subjective impulse
in Hopkins was intense, encouraged by frequent introspection and often painful self-analysis, but usually turned
to serve a larger religious purpose. The first section of "The

Wreck of the Deutschland" is directly autobiographical, an account of the poet's experience of spiritual "instress," which is intended to foreshadow the theme of the second part, the hope for the total conversion of England through the example of the transfigured drowning nun. The nature poems that followed record the warmly personal, yet essentially selfless response of the "heart in hiding" to the intricate inscaped beauty of created things. Even among the "terrible sonnets" only one remains narrowly and specifically private: "To seem the stranger lies my lot," the pathetic cry of loneliness, touched by self-pity, from exile in Ireland. The others, especially in the sestets, become powerful statements of human struggle and religious resolution, for they succeed in relating the most personal of alarms to the general plight of mankind:

> O the mind, mind has mountains; cliffs of fall
> Frightful, sheer, no-man-fathomed. Hold them cheap
> May who ne'er hung there. Nor does long our small
> Durance deal with that steep or deep. Here! creep,
> Wretch, under a comfort serves in a whirlwind: all
> Life death does end and each day dies with sleep.

To Hopkins controlled self-awareness may be the prelude to conversion. To George Meredith self-consciousness of any kind is forever fraught with peril. Though based on his own tragic first marriage, which ended with his wife's desertion and suicide, Meredith's *Modern Love* places its intimate autobiographical content at a steady impersonal distance. As the title suggests, the poem concerns not a unique mismarriage, but a typical "modern" relationship. The husband, who is described in the third person and speaks in the first, is irritable in his defensive sarcasm, self-dramatizing, inconsiderate. The wife in turn is sentimental, vain, and vulnerable. Yet neither is the villain; "passions spin the plot"; both are "betrayed by what is false within." No less than the absurd Sir Willoughby Patterne, though they play grimmer roles, they are both egoists, lacking in the comic spirit, failing sadly in perspective. Both refuse to accept the challenge of change and maturity; they have "fed not on the advancing hours"; they childishly take offense, mistrust each other, and seek self-justification at disastrous cost:

> Then each applied to each that fatal knife,
> Deep questioning, which probes to endless dole.
> Ah, what a dusty answer gets the soul
> When hot for certainties in this our life!

Like these lost lovers, most modern men and women, Meredith would have us believe, are corrupted by the principle of self and an isolating pride. Few dare enter his enchanted Woods of Westermain, where the abundant life flourishes only when it has learned to repel "the scaly Dragon-fowl" that is egoism. But even poets scarcely attain Meredith's selfless ideal (which is similar to Edwin Muir's impersonal "nature") with the grace or purity of his "lark ascending," whose song remains "seraphically free / Of taint of personality."

"Shall I sonnet-sing you about myself?" asks Robert Browning contemptuously in a late lyric called "House"—referring not, of course, to Elizabeth Barrett's sonnet-singing, but to Rossetti's *House of Life*, which he considered shamelessly subjective. Browning was no less eager than other Victorians to achieve self-expression; he was simply more reluctant than most, even than Tennyson, to reveal anything of his private life to an inquisitive public. In his monologues he maintains a persistent interest in the vivid personalities of egoists and casuists, madmen and gentle philosophers, all intent upon confession, introspection, apologia, or self-analysis. And his speakers are not to be taken—or mistaken—for his spokesmen. Many, in fact, do voice his values, his ideal of aspiring struggle, his cult of imperfection, his notions of faith and doubt, courage and cowardice; and all demand some close confrontation of the problems of selfhood and identity.[15] But the dramatic form provides a means of insinuating points of view without the risk of overt or definite commitment. It offers the poet a desired protection and concealment, a way of *hiding* his private life and subjective emotions. And if we remember that the word *hide* ultimately derives from the same root as *house* and *hoard*, a house being a hiding place or secret hoard, we begin to appreciate the implications of one of Browning's most characteristic metaphors.

"House" develops in explicit detail the image of poetry as private housing:

> Shall I sonnet-sing you about myself?
>   Do I live in a house you would like to see?
> Is it scant of gear, has it store of pelf?
>   "Unlock my heart with a sonnet-key?"
>
> Invite the world, as my betters have done?
>   "Take notice: this building remains on view,
> Its suites of reception every one,
>   Its private apartment and bedroom too;
>
> "For a ticket, apply to the Publisher."
>   No: thanking the public, I must decline.
> A peep through my window, if folk prefer;
>   But, please you, no foot over threshold of mine!

The poem then illustrates its argument with an account of an actual house in Italy, destroyed by an earthquake and so exposed to the malicious gossip of the townsmen, who never before had an intimate view of the dead owner's personal habits. The poet, however, intervenes: whatever may be said in disparagement, "the goodman of the house at least / Kept house to himself till an earthquake came." The moral is only too clear; the poet, denying public access to his threshold, must resolutely reject Wordsworth's assumption that the great objective Shakespeare himself wrote subjectively in his sonnets and so in effect invited an invasion of his innermost chambers:

> "Hoity toity! A street to explore,
>   Your house the exception! '*With this same key*
> *Shakespeare unlocked his heart,*' once more!"
>   Did Shakespeare? If so, the less Shakespeare he!

Much of Browning's 1876 volume, *Pacchiarotto and How He Worked in Distemper,* in which "House" appeared, is concerned with related themes: the poet's response to his audience and every man's right to privacy. Several pieces repeat with variations the image of the house. "Shop" rebukes a tradesman who, living with his wares, has no other house, no escape from his public business, and so no second life of his own. "Fears and Scruples" imagines God as a friend hidden from view behind brick walls, spying on the world through shutters. "A Forgiveness" presents a proud autocrat who from boyhood has retired to a secret room in his large house, "my fortress, stronghold from annoy, / Proof-positive of ownership," which finally becomes a paranoid's refuge,

> My closet of entrenchment to withstand
> Invasion of the foe on every hand.

And the curious title poem with grotesque rhymes and blunt invective attacks all critics guilty of "bringing more filth into my house / Than ever you found there" and especially, through the tale of a third-rate Italian painter turned polemicist, the poetaster Alfred Austin, who had recently in a distempered article questioned Browning's capacity and status.[16] More accessibly, without the house image, the lyrical monologue "At the Mermaid" permits Shakespeare himself, sounding remarkably like Robert Browning, to defend the logic of the locked heart, of a poet's refusing to divulge his personal tastes or otherwise to "sell you cheap" his soul:

> Which of you did I enable
>   Once to slip inside my breast,
> There to catalogue and label
>   What I like least, what love best,
> Hope and fear, believe and doubt of,
>   Seek and shun, respect—deride?
> Who has right to make a rout of
>   Rarities he found inside?

Browning's impatience with readers looking for personal confession in his work undoubtedly increased with his growing reputation. In the 1870s, when the legend of the Wimpole Street romance was beginning to take shape, he was particularly irked by biographers in search of details about his courtship and marriage. But twenty years earlier he was already intent on declaring his objectivity. In the epilogue to *Men and Women*, "One Word More," addressed to Mrs. Browning, he begs leave to "speak this once in my true person," and this once simply to offer the labors of his "brain" to the woman who commands his "heart." The other fifty poems of the volume are to be construed as dramatic and disinterested, for

> Hardly shall I tell my joys and sorrows,
> Hopes and fears, belief and disbelieving:
> I am mine and yours—the rest be all men's.

One of the fifty, "How It Strikes a Contemporary," a monologue spoken by a Spanish man of affairs, describes the town poet of Valladolid. Observant of life in all its variety and color, "Scenting the world, looking it full in face," the poet is "The town's true master if the town but knew." Yet all the time he remains aloof from the crowd, unobtrusive, and, contrary to vulgar gossip, thoroughly abstemious in his habits; he lives neither as a princely sybarite nor as a garreted bohemian, but with unromantic respectability

> In that new stuccoed third house by the bridge,
> Fresh-painted, rather smart than otherwise!

Like other pieces in *Men and Women*, the poem is placed at some distance in space and time, as if to disown immediate identification, but the poet-realist at its center, in his un-invaded middle-class house, comes obviously close to the ideal impersonal artist Browning himself in his maturity aspired to be.[17]

The younger Browning, however, had not been so alarmed at the prospect of self-revelation. There is little dramatic hiding or "housekeeping" in his first volume. Subtitled "A Fragment of a Confession," *Pauline* is an amorphous Shelleyan rhapsody, mildly erotic, wildly undisciplined in its subjectivity, a glorification of the lonely ego and its wavering moods, its adolescent fears of love and death and its broad declarations of faith and doubt. John Stuart Mill, who annotated a review copy, properly detected a high degree of disorganized autobiography and concluded that "the writer seem[ed] possessed with a more intense and morbid self-consciousness than I ever knew in any sane man."[18] Carefully weighing and partially accepting the charge, Browning resolved to write no more of himself directly but always to make his poetry the dramatic speech of "so many persons, not mine." Yet the impulse to justify his views never wholly vanished, and more than the "once" of "One Word More" he faltered in his objective resolution. He made clear enough in lyrics throughout his career what he liked least and loved best, and in some longer pieces he argued, often with characteristic involution and verbosity, the wisdom of his choices and convictions. *Christmas Eve and Easter Day*, for instance, which appeared less than two months before *In Memoriam* and stands in sharp contrast to it as a religious testimony, defends at length his preference of English Dissent to Roman Catholicism and German Higher Criticism and debates the sanctions of his own brand of evangelical Christianity. Nearly forty years later *Parleyings with Certain People of Importance in Their Day* allows Browning, in his own voice and a singularly awkward syntax, to harangue seven more or less forgotten men representing seven of his principal concerns, and in the process to present what amounts to his intellectual autobiography.[19] But the personal ideas expounded in such pieces are less engaging or original than the poet must have supposed, and the artistry falls far short of that achieved in his best dramatic monologues. Browning need not have proclaimed so loudly his need for concealment. Few of his true admirers could regret that he did not choose more frequently to open his private house for public inspection.

Though often more indebted to the major Victorians than they cared to admit, the principal proponents of the modernist mode in the early twentieth century devised their own techniques of concealing or transmuting the subjective impulse and developed a new vocabulary to affirm the autonomy of their art. Ezra Pound alone freely acknowledged the influence of Browning, but many others experimented as he did with variations on the dramatic monologue and with the lyric as essentially dramatic speech rather than the poet's personal cry. T. S. Eliot, demanding an adequate "objective correlative," exploited odd juxtapositions of image, disjunctions of syntax, irony, wit, sharpened metaphor, and recondite allusion. Wallace Stevens, devoted to his "supreme fictions" and intricate artifice, practiced a fastidious hard-edged depersonalized aestheticism. And Yeats, in whom the subjective compulsion was stronger and more passionate, sought to find not the self but an "image," a complementary mask:

> I call to the mysterious one who yet
> Shall walk the wet sands by the edge of the stream
> And look most like me, being indeed my double,
> And prove of all imaginable things
> The most unlike, being my anti-self.[20]

For all these and many others distrustful of naked personality in art, C. S. Lewis provided a sanction in his attack on "the personal heresy." "To see things as the poet sees them," Lewis argued, "I must share his consciousness and not attend to it; I must look where he looks and not turn round to face him. I must make him not a spectacle but a pair of spectacles."[21]

By the 1960s, however, the modernist movement was inspiring scant respect among writers of a younger generation responsive to the claims of a "counter-culture" and perplexed about their own function and identity in a world more desperate and threatening than any intellectual Waste Land. To many of these the austere objective poetry of the age of Eliot seemed already remote in its calculated cleverness and disengagement. Whether or not they wished to make "a spectacle" of themselves, the new poets cultivated a confessional verse, often invertebrate in form, frequently embarrassing in its intimacies, and more self-regarding than the work of the most subjective Romantics.

W. H. Auden was never a "confessional poet," in the contemporary sense of that label. As a distinguished exponent of poetic modernism, he had no desire for apology, clinical self-analysis, or defiant exhibition. Yet his own late work in its own way seemed to recognize the "post-modern" thrust towards subjectivity, for in it he had moved from the brittle brilliance of his early satires to a relaxed and gentle introspection. His 1965 *About the House* offers what Browning's "House" refused to allow, a view of his private residence and its personal furniture. Among the constituent poems, the moving elegy to Louis MacNeice, "The Cave of Making," which unlocks the poet's workroom-study, reveals

> how much, in our lonely dens, we need the companionship
>   of our good dead, to give us
> comfort on dowly days when the self is a nonentity
>   dumped on a mound of nothing.[22]

The "I" of the speaker, though clearly Auden, here becomes, as often in Tennyson's poetry, a warmly felt first person plural, the voice of the human condition, and the den poem as a result becomes far more than "this egocentric monologue" (as the ending self-consciously describes it). So

it is throughout the house; we are invited to share an interpretation of our common experience. The poet admits his
readers to room after room, while he himself stands con-
fidingly at the door of each, as if inviting the guests to turn
round to face him. If he has no lurid secrets to divulge,
neither has he any trace of Browning's anxious fear of disclosure.

ᵛᵍ VIII ᵍᵛ

PERSONAL STATEMENTS

To confess, Yes I remember. Perhaps even to have
a voice. To murmur, Yes I remember. What an
addition to company that would be! A voice in the
first person singular. Murmuring now and then,
Yes I remember.

—*Samuel Beckett*

S CRUPULOUSLY edited in its several versions, Wordsworth's *Prelude* has at last taken its place as the archetypal
subjective poem in the language. Shortly before his death
in 1977 Robert Lowell, with a gesture of indebtedness,
described the drift of his own life's work: "The thread that
strings it all together is my autobiography, it is a small-
scale *Prelude*, written in many different styles, and with
digressions, yet a continuing story."[1] But the level of self-
revelation in Lowell's poetry, and in much other contemporary verse, differs sharply from Wordsworth's discreet
testimony of spiritual growth in a world of ordinary sights
and shared responses, for in it the assertion of an intensely
private suffering has replaced the assured subjective discovery of a general psychology.

Though anticipated by Allen Ginsberg's rowdier effusions, Lowell's *Life Studies* of 1959, more than any other
volume, set the vogue for American "confessional" poetry
of the 'sixties.[2] Always the anxious craftsman, Lowell worked

and reworked his autobiographical probings to achieve economy and tautness of line and image and an often wry view of the traumas he was exploring. Yet self-absorption inevitably invaded his detachment, and his friend, Allen Tate, who had greatly admired his early work, understandably complained to him of the later personal pieces: "The new ones sound to me like messages to yourself. . . . Quite bluntly, these details, presented in causerie and at random, are of interest only to you." Lowell, nonetheless, persisted, seeking for his intimate messages an apparently relaxed idiom, "one that used images and ironic or amusing particulars."[3] Lesser "confessional" poets, some of whom resented and rejected that label,[4] were content to deliver their undramatic monologues in an "authentic" speech form, unliterary, explosive, consciously raw, sometimes ostentatiously vulgar. Many, unlike Lowell, were more intent on a personal statement than a personal style.

Whatever its aesthetic virtues or defects, confessional poetry, far more than Arnold's "Empedocles on Etna," offers everything to endure and little to inspirit. Much of its concern, even among its most gifted exponents—Theodore Roethke, Sylvia Plath, Lowell himself—centers on the torments of nervous instability, especially the cycles of manic depression. Whether the "I" of the poem is speaking of actual fact or of fantasy, the autobiography, as presented, repeatedly proves a record of threatened sexuality, psychic disorientation, and suicidal despair. Lowell revealed more than we need rightly know of his failures in marriage, his extramarital affairs, his reactions to those closest to him, and his own recurrent mental distress—all in a restricted first person and all apparently "real," for the telling bears no mark of fiction or subterfuge. John Berryman, on the other hand, invented a third person for his "Dream Songs,"

an alcoholic masochist named "Henry," but Henry's neu-
roses are so like what we readily recognize as Berryman's
own that we must doubt both the purpose and the substance
of the persona. Confessional verses are frequently poems
about the self writing poems as a means of release or ther-
apy. In *Day by Day*, his last volume, some of which reaffirms
a lost objectivity, Lowell questions his self-reflexive work,
his effort to give "my simple autobiography a plot," and his
search for order when the "blessed structures, plot and
rhyme," seem to have failed him:

> Is getting well ever an art,
> Or art a way to get well?[5]

But the content of such poetry, whether Lowell's or Berryman's, may well deflect the reader's attention from the
poetic process to the illness under treatment or review, and
so threaten to engage his appetite for mere gossip or eaves-
dropping, or at worst a prurient voyeurism, an unpoetic
defense perhaps against the spectacle of pain and madness.
Despite flashes of vivid metaphor and interludes of bright-
ening irony, poem after confessional poem remains a dark
testament to unbalance and self-destructive compulsion. In
such terms autobiography, once the search for coherence
and meaning, becomes troubled case-history, the disaffected poet's rejection of Wordsworth's ordinary universe.

Confessional verse has, of course, been only one kind of
recent poetry, and not the only or always the best kind
written by the confessional poets. Yet it is nonetheless a
striking illustration of the persistence and often extravagant
indulgence of the subjective impulse. In the visual arts,
where direct autobiography is less to be expected, the near-
est parallel is the occasional intimate self-portrait or the

lacerating self-caricature. (An early modern example of both may be found in Stanley Spencer's study, now at the Tate Gallery, of himself in grotesque nudity contemplating his recumbent wife.) But the personal statement, when graphic or tactile, requires no such narrative context; calculated novelty of approach or material may be all that is necessary. The statement may assume any form sufficient to demonstrate the artist's individual difference, isolation from common values, and revolt from established aesthetic traditions. It frequently consists of unlikely configurations or enigmatic vacancies: a torn canvas tacked to a barn board, an empty frame, a reputedly buried sculpture, random strings crisscrossing an egg-crate, a stone wrapped in burlap or a whole rocky coastline shrouded in plastic, parings of fingernails or other unconsecrated personal relics.

None of these "statements," except the biological exhibits, seems patently insane, and each to the artist, if indeed it is more than an exercise in labored exuberance, may have some real esoteric meaning. But to the spectator the display exists all too often simply to announce the defiance or eccentricity of an elusive alienated self. None invites measurement by any recognizable aesthetic standard. Whatever its appeal, each exhibition stands anarchically alone, never to be repeated, with no relation to a canon or a developing technique. None in any true sense evinces an earned style or bears a real signature. The personal statement, at least of this kind, denies not only the "nature" that Edwin Muir admired, but even personality itself, which demands some measure of continuity, complexity, and social interplay.

An obvious sanction for the unconventional artifact has been the violence and unreason of a society offensive in many respects to every sensitive observer. But a more specific rationale for alienation in both art and literature appeared throughout the nineteen sixties and early 'seventies in the prose and verse of R. D. Laing, who became a sort of guru-prophet of the counter-culture.[6] Laing as psychologist moved from a close clinical description of schizophrenia to a virtual endorsement of the schizoid condition as one effective means of resisting and resolving the discontents of modern civilization. The schizophrenic, according to Laing, may have embarked on a "healing voyage" away from the constraints of family, social institutions, and every objective "otherness" that threatens the sanctity of the subjective life. Schizophrenia in such terms might be less an illness than a commendable strategy of escape and recovery, a declaration of "authentic" personal need. So by extension might be other rather different pathologies—manic depression, for example, or narcissism—insofar as they encouraged radical self-absorption as a release from social engagement.

No English or American writer or artist is a more conspicuous representative of the actual schizophrenic as autobiographer than the Swiss Adolf Wölfli, who was certified as insane, incarcerated for thirty-five years, and ultimately in 1975, long after his death, celebrated by a Wölfli Foundation dedicated to the study and promotion of his work.[7] During his confinement Wölfli devoted much frightening energy to imagining self-histories, which he told in elaborate drawings and accompanying narrative commentary: first the fantasies of the child Doufi, *From the Cradle to the Grave*, and later the celebration of a new-found self, "Saint Adolf II." From the beginning he chose to cover every square inch of paper with symbols and hieroglyphs, haunted eyes, hooded faces, talking vegetables, images of space travel, dizzying architectural perspectives, musical notations, calculations of enormous financial returns on Adolf's fancied investments.

Whether his madness released or merely distorted an impressive talent, Wölfli's designs, especially his mandalas and abstract geometries, attracted the attention, even during his lifetime, of commercial dealers and buyers. But despite its often meticulous rhythm, his production in both line and language testifies as much to his sickness as to his skill. The detail of a late picture, "Saint Mary with the Christ-Child; That is, with my Humble Self, St. Adolf II," does nothing to conceal the messianic delusion. Here and elsewhere his obsessions perpetually intrude upon our disinterested view of his subjective art.

Wölfli's example may well seem remote and extreme. But within the English context and with a more persuasive sanity of logic, Adrian Stokes also drew upon the schizophrenic sense of otherness, in a determined effort to "rationalize" the distorted vision. Published in 1947 but little known till a generation later when Laing and others may have prepared an audience for it, Stokes's *Inside Out* evokes childhood memories of perception and fantasy in a wholly existential Hyde Park and Kensington Gardens. After prolonged psychoanalysis Stokes the autobiographer has come to accept and value his subjective responses to a large amorphous outside space as expressing his need to project himself upon the environment and so to objectify his deepest emotions by way of aesthetic substitution. He is eager to defend what Ruskin attacked as the pathetic fallacy, for "indeed," he writes, "it is the initial imputation, in such a strong degree, of emotional states to the external world, inferno or paradiso or both at once, which characterizes the person who will primarily be an artist, even when childhood is passed." Some such imputation, as Stokes understands it, becomes the essential mark of all humanity: "Whatever the degree, whatever the distortion, all men impute themselves to their surroundings. The broad distorted aspect of the innermost informs every particle of the huge outlying space."[8] *Inside Out* moves accordingly from an intensely private experience to a generalized aesthetic theory. Beginning with the bemused child in the park, it concludes with a close appreciation of Cézanne's spatial blockings, the splendid substitutions of a creative mind.

Few autobiographers have succeeded as well as Stokes in identifying, transcending, and sublimating a neurosis. But many since the early modern period have been only too self-consciously aware of their psychological case-histories. Some, with traces of an older reticence, have confessed sadly to aberration or instability. G. Lowes Dickinson, for instance, in reminiscences first published some forty years after his death in 1932, set out "to tell what is usually not told"—that is, solemnly to reveal behind the facade of respectability a secret life of fetishes, delight in self-inflicted pain, and furtive homosexuality.[9] Others, less inhibited, have freely presented their fixations as tokens of temperament and sensibility. And some have emulated the bravado of Henry Miller, who with due irony, at the beginning of his earliest novel of self-contemplation, announced: "I have moved the typewriter into the next room where I can see myself in the mirror as I write."[10]

No one, however, in sustained psychological self-scrutiny, has surpassed—or apparently desired to reach—the self-loathing achieved by Michel Leiris. *La Règle du jeu*, begun in 1935 when Leiris was thirty-four, "at life's midpoint," and translated in the 1960s as *Manhood: A Journey from Childhood into the Fierce Order of Virility*, has received wide recognition in England and America as an uncompromising personal statement, a ruthless exercise in self-exposure. *Manhood* avows sadomasochism, voyeurism, trans-

vestism, erotic perversities, recurrent impotence, the crav-
ing for self-degradation, and the transitory thrills of a guilt
complex. The author appears the narcissist reversed: "I loathe
unexpectedly catching sight of myself in the mirror, for
unless I have prepared myself for the confrontation, I seem
humiliatingly ugly to myself each time." He calls attempted
suicide the "punishment one inflicts on oneself in order to
have the right to love oneself to excess," and he describes
a manic assault with sharp scissors on his whole naked body.
He claims a fearful attraction to women weeping, for he
"cannot conceive of love save in torment and tears." Having
told his mistress, "I'd like us to be buried together," he
comments on that expression of affection: "This sentence
must be one of the most genuinely tender I have ever spoken
to anyone." At times his wicked attitudinizing seems as
ludicrous as the young George Moore's: "As for Biblical
antiquity," he declares, "I never can think without emotion
of Sodom and Gomorrah." But there is little of Moore's
ebullience in the neurasthenic virilist, who finds the passage
to manhood only a steady depletion of vital energy. In an
"Afterword" Leiris explains his cruel self-violation as an
effort to rid himself of "certain agonizing images" and to
find somewhere through complete confession some absolution. Professional psychotherapy, to which he has re-
sorted, has, he assures us, provided but little satisfaction
or relief. Yet the record he has assembled remains the exhibition of a mind in need of psychiatric help, rather than
an exploration of the devious paths by which a representative man found his own way to maturity.[11]

If the new autobiography as a genre has exploited the ills
of the psyche and the maladies of maladjustment, it has
also, with a characteristic contemporary distrust of language, questioned the whole process of self-creation through

words, the actual substance of memory, and indeed the very reality of selfhood. The best and most cogent example of this latter development may well be Samuel Beckett's late, elegiac *Company* (1980). Here the author, or a speaker much like him, offers a few sudden glimpses of things past, snapshots, as it were, of his childhood in Ireland, his dependence on mother and father, his solitary rambles as a boy, a shadowy early love affair. Then almost at once, in the very act of recollection, he retreats, wondering how accurate could be his remembrance. Might his past self, he asks, be simply a fable, a figment of imagination invented to solace a lonely present? An actual past self, he muses, would surely be welcome "company," the alter ego for which the mind now yearns in an encompassing dark. But there is now no certain personal identity in the present, nor any true community with another in all past time: "For the first person singular and a fortiori plural pronoun had never any place in your vocabulary." All that now preoccupies the speaker is his physical isolation, the body prone, scarcely moving, and always, as the ending emphasizes, always quite "Alone." Thus the subjective impulse subsides in ultimate despair,

Till finally you hear how words are coming to an end. With every inane word a little nearer to the last. And how the fable too. The fable of one with you in the dark, the fable of one fabling of one with you in the dark.[12]

With Beckett the personal statement, in a distinctly personal style, moves beyond private reflection to become a bleak paradigm of the condition of modern man. The key of subjectivity that T. S. Eliot heard turning nearly sixty years earlier has now effectively locked in the prisoner of self, and no outside voices penetrate the thick-walled containment. But *Company*, firm as it is in its finality, does not necessarily terminate the autobiographical genre. The same key, as many have discovered in the past two centuries, can open as well as close the door to dialogue between the self and the objective ordinary world. Neither the distance of one from the other nor the frequent antagonism has required a categorical denial of either.

Among all the autobiographers we have encountered Wordsworth seems best to have understood the need for a reciprocal relation between the inner and the outer. Near the end of *The Prelude* he describes the vision by which his subjective art, including that poem itself, was to be shaped:

> I remember well
> That in life's every-day appearances
> I seemed about this time to gain clear sight
> Of a new world—a world, too, that was fit
> To be transmitted, and to other eyes
> Made visible as ruled by those fixed laws
> Whence spiritual dignity originates,
> Which do both give it being, and maintain
> A balance, an ennobling interchange
> Of action from without and from within,
> The excellence, pure function, and best power
> Both of the object seen and eye that sees.[13]

Ever since Rousseau and the first Romantics faith in the subjective life has been an essential defense against a soul-destroying objectivism. At the same time the sense of a reality beyond the self has steadily challenged an isolating solipsism. From the beginning the literature of selfhood, both animated and threatened by its focus, has sought in its every positive aspiration a Wordsworthian balance between self and society, and at its rare best has achieved a rich, ennobling interchange.

NOTES

I. THE UNPRECEDENTED SELF

1. Carlyle, *The Life of John Sterling* (1851), Chap. VIII, "Coleridge."
2. Coleridge, *Biographia Literaria*, Chap. X. Cf. De Quincey's footnote to the 1856 edition of his *Confessions of an English Opium-Eater* (Part III): " 'Objective.'—This word, so nearly unintelligible in 1821, so intensely scholastic, and, consequently, when surrounded by familiar and vernacular words, so apparently pedantic, yet, on the other hand, so indispensable to accurate thinking, and to *wide* thinking, has since 1821 become too common to need any apology."
3. Coleridge, "Table Talk," May 12, 1830, *Complete Works*, 7 vols. (New York: Harper, 1884), VI, 312.
4. Alfred McKinley Terhune and Annabelle Burdick Terhune, eds., *The Letters of Edward FitzGerald*, 4 vols. (Princeton, N.J.: Princeton University Press, 1980), I, 250, 528 (letters of June 7, 1840, and March, 1846).
5. "H.M.S. Pinafore," *The Complete Plays of Gilbert and Sullivan* (Garden City, N.Y.: Garden City Publishing Co., 1941), p. 100.
6. Wordsworth, letter of May 1, 1805, in Philip Wayne, ed., *Letters of William Wordsworth* (London: Oxford University Press, 1954), p. 72.
7. P. P. Howe, ed., *Complete Words of William Hazlitt*, Centenary Edition, 21 vols. (London: Dent, 1930–34), VIII, 44.
8. Erik H. Erikson, *Identity, Youth and Crisis* (New York: Norton, 1968), p. 43.
9. Emerson, "Life and Letters in New England," *Complete Works of Ralph Waldo Emerson*, Centenary Edition, 12 vols. (Boston: Houghton Mifflin, 1903–1904), X, 326, 329. The passage was called to my attention by Kenneth Marc Harris.
10. Hopkins, "As kingfishers catch fire," in W. H. Gardner and N. H. MacKenzie, eds., *The Poems of Gerard Manley Hopkins* (London: Oxford University Press, 1970), p. 90.

11. Hopkins, "Spiritual Exercise," August 20, 1880, John Pick, ed., *A Hopkins Reader* (Garden City, N.Y.: Doubleday, 1966), pp. 396–397.

12. Pater, "Prosper Mérimée," *Miscellaneous Studies, Works of Walter Pater*, 8 vols. (London: Macmillan, 1901), VIII, 12.

13. Pater, "Charles Lamb," *Appreciations, Works*, V, 117.

14. Pater, *Marius the Epicurean* (Chap. XXV), *Works*, III, 173.

15. Wilde, *Intentions*, in Richard Ellmann, ed., *The Artist as Critic: Critical Writings of Oscar Wilde* (New York: Random House, 1969), p. 389.

16. Eliot, *Collected Poems, 1900–1935* (New York: Harcourt Brace, 1936), pp. 97–98. Eliot's image of the prison, though adapted from Dante, and Bradley's closed circle both recall, more than Eliot or Bradley might have wished, Pater's "Conclusion" to *The Renaissance:* "Experience . . . is ringed round for each of us by that thick wall of personality through which no real voice has ever pierced on its way to us, or from us to that which we can only conjecture to be without. Every one of those impressions is the impression of the individual in his isolation, each mind keeping as a solitary prisoner its own dream of a world."

17. As an example of the hermeneutic approach, see Frank Kermode, *The Genesis of Secrecy: On the Interpretation of Narrative* (Cambridge, Mass: Harvard University Press, 1979), and the questioning review of the same by E. D. Hirsch, Jr., *The New York Review*, 26, no. 10 (1979), 18–20.

18. Wilde, pp. 365–366.

19. Coleridge on *Hamlet*, in Thomas M. Raysor, ed., *Coleridge's Shakespearean Criticism*, 2 vols. (Cambridge, Mass: Harvard University Press, 1930), II, 192; see also I, 38–40, II, 272–273.

20. Arnold, preface of 1853 to his *Poems*.

21. Bagehot, "Wordsworth, Tennyson, and Browning," in Norman St John-Stevas, ed., *The Collected Works of Walter Bagehot*, 7 vols. (Cambridge, Mass: Harvard University Press, 1965), II, 352; cf. I, 164–165: "In fact, it would appear that the tendency to, and the faculty for, self-delineation, are very closely connected with the dreaminess of disposition and impotence of character which we spoke of just now [i.e., in reference to Coleridge]. Persons very subject to these can grasp no external object, comprehend no external being, and therefore they are left to themselves. Their own character is the only one which they can view as a whole, or depict as a reality."

22. William Hale White ("Mark Rutherford"), *Pages from a Journal* (London: Oxford University Press, 1930), p. 343.

23. Lawrence, on *Hamlet*, in Anthony Beal, ed., *D. H. Lawrence: Selected Literary Criticism* (New York: Viking, 1966), p. 276 (other references, *passim*); and on the colloquy with the "skeleton," in Edward D.

Macdonald, ed., *Phoenix: The Posthumous Papers of D. H. Lawrence* (New York: Viking, 1936), p. 736.

24. Russell, *The Autobiography of Bertrand Russell, 1872–1914* (Boston: Little Brown, 1967), p. 286.

25. Newman, *Parochial and Plain Sermons*, 8 vols. (London: Longmans Green, 1894), I, 42–43. But such assumptions about a common human nature were much rarer in Newman's time than in Pope's.

26. Goethe, quoted from a conversation with Eckermann by John O. Lyons, *The Invention of the Self* (Carbondale, Ill.: Southern Illinois University Press, 1978), p. 218.

27. Cf. Lyons, p. 203. Lyons subtitles his able and suggestive book "The Hinge of Consciousness in the Eighteenth Century." I am indebted to him for many aperçus of great interest to me in my study of later periods.

28. There is perhaps a hint of this conclusion in the third line of the first stanza, where Cowper speaks of "such a destined wretch as I," but at that point we assume that Cowper is alluding to general human destiny and man's capacity for pain, rather than to his own experience. For the next fifty-seven lines, at any rate, we concentrate attention on the drowned sailor.

29. Lyons, p. 16, and for more specific evidence, see pp. 1–39.

30. See Alexander Bain, *The Senses and the Intellect* (London: Parker, 1855), esp. pp. 315–450; later editions (1864, 1868) amplify the theory of "retention."

31. Mill, *An Examination of Sir William Hamilton's Philosophy*, 3rd ed. (London: Longmans, 1867), pp. 241, 242, 254, 256.

32. Carlyle, *Sartor Resartus* ("Natural Supernaturalism" and "The Everlasting No").

33. Carlyle, "Signs of the Times" (1829), which contrasts the Mechanical and the Dynamical.

34. Carlyle, on Goethe, preface (1824) to his translation of *Wilhelm Meister;* on Shakespeare (1828), *Works*, 30 vols. (New York: Scribner, 1896–1901), XXVI, 203. See also "Prospective," *Sartor Resartus*.

35. Parts of Franklin's autobiography were published under other titles in 1793 and 1818. The Yale University Press edition (1964) of the *Autobiography* provides much detail describing its complicated bibliographical history.

36. *The Monthly Review*, 2nd Series, 29 (1797), 375. Cited as the earliest example of the term in the 1972 Supplement to the *OED*. The author is identified as William Taylor of Norwich by Benjamin Christie Nangle, *The Monthly Review, Second Series, 1790–1815: Indexes of Contributors and Articles* (Oxford: Clarendon Press, 1955), p. 113, Item 936. The

OED had previously cited Southey's use in 1809. Coleridge speaks of Wordsworth's "divine Self-biography," in Kathleen Coburn, ed., *The Notebooks of Samuel Taylor Coleridge*, 2 vols. (New York: Pantheon Books, 1957) I, #1801.

37. Southey, "Portugueze [*sic*] Literature," *Quarterly Review*, 1 (1809), 283.

38. See Richard D. Altick, *Lives and Letters* (New York: Knopf, 1965), p. 104. Limiting the focus to the poets, Altick tells us, "Before 1800, only nine English poets wrote autobiographies that survive; between 1800 and 1900 at least forty-two wrote such accounts."

II. TOWARDS AUTOBIOGRAPHY

1. Jacques Lacan, trans. Anthony Wilden, *The Language of the Self* (Baltimore: The Johns Hopkins University Press, 1968), p. 84.

2. See Georg Misch, *A History of Autobiography in Antiquity*, 2 vols. (London: Routledge and Kegan Paul, 1950); Misch fully identifies the attitudes in antiquity working against the autobiographical mode.

3. *The Confessions of St. Augustine*, trans. John K. Ryan (Garden City: Image Books, 1960), p. 67.

4. P. 202.

5. P. 250.

6. Pp. 236–238, 246.

7. See John F. Benton, "Consciousness of Self and 'Personality' in the Renaissance of the Twelfth Century," a working paper for a conference of November 1977, sponsored by U.C.L.A. and the Mediaeval Academy of America.

8. See Margaret Bottrall, *Every Man a Phoenix: Studies in Seventeenth-century Autobiography* (London: Murray, 1958), "autobiography" here being more a method than a form.

9. John Bunyan, *Grace Abounding to the Chief of Sinners* (Oxford: Clarendon Press, 1962), p. 5.

10. Sir Thomas Browne, *The Religio Medici and Other Writings* (London: Dent, 1906), pp. 2, 81, 83.

11. Walter Kaiser, ed., *Selected Essays of Montaigne* (Boston: Houghton Mifflin, 1964), pp. 2, 347, 350, 387. See also Kaiser's excellent introduction. Cf. Richard L. Regosin, *The Matter of My Book: Montaigne's Essais as the Book of the Self* (Berkeley, University of California Press, 1977).

12. See Georges Gusdorf, "Conditions et limites de l'autobiographie," in Günter Reichenkron, ed., *Formen der Selbstdarstellung* (Berlin: Duncker u. Humblot, 1956), pp. 105–123. Also cited by Lyons, p. 69.

13. Cf. Lyons, p. 43.

14. William L. Howarth comments on Rembrandt, "In his lifetime Rembrandt painted over a hundred self-portraits, seventy of them full studies. Viewed as a whole, they form a serial image, like frames in a strip of movie film." Howarth, "Some Principles of Autobiography," in James Olney, *Autobiography: Essays Theoretical and Critical* (Princeton, N.J.: Princeton University Press, 1980), p. 104.

15. Blake, "Florentine Ingratitude," Marginalia from the Nonesuch Edition, reprinted in *The Complete Poetry . . . of John Donne and The Complete Poetry of William Blake* (New York: Random House, 1941), p. 1043.

16. The Hogarth and the Kauffman to which I refer are in the National Portrait Gallery, London, along with a number of other eighteenth-century self-portraits by (to cite but a few) George Stubbs, Joseph Wright of Derby, John Opie, Allan Ramsay, and George Romney. Hogarth and Reynolds also did other self-portraits than the ones I mention. Joan Kinneir has edited a volume of self-portrait drawings from various periods and countries, *The Artist by Himself* (New York: St. Martin's Press, 1980).

17. Samuel Johnson, *Idler*, No. 84, November 24, 1759, in W. J. Bate, John M. Bullitt, and L. F. Powell, eds., *The Idler and The Adventurer* (New Haven: Yale University Press, 1963), pp. 263–264.

18. Isaac D'Israeli, "Some Observations on Diaries, Self-biography, and Self-characters," *Miscellanies: or, Literary Recreations* (London: Cadell and Davies, 1796), pp. 95–110.

19. *The Life of David Hume, Esq., Written by Himself* (London: Strahan and Cadell, 1777), p. 6. To this autobiography, posthumously published, Adam Smith appended a letter describing Hume's stoic courage as he lay dying.

20. Edward Gibbon, *Memoirs of My Life and Writings* (London: 1796), pp. 2, 43, 84, 89, 150.

21. Mark Pattison, *Memoirs* (London: Macmillan, 1885), pp. 2, 129–130, 331. Actually, however, though Rousseau was widely read in Victorian England, he was not widely imitated. Phyllis Grosskurth discusses the problem in "Where Was Rousseau?" in George P. Landow, ed., *Approaches to Victorian Autobiography* (Athens, Ohio: Ohio University Press, 1979), pp. 26–38.

22. Johnson on Rousseau, in G. B. Hill, ed., *Boswell's Life of Johnson*, 6 vols. (Oxford: Clarendon Press, 1934), II, 12. On Burke and Rousseau, see J. H. Huizinga, *Rousseau: The Self-made Saint* (New York: Grossman, 1976), p. 249; Walpole and Hume on Rousseau: Matthew Josephson, *Jean-Jacques Rousseau* (New York: Harcourt Brace, 1931), pp. 447–468; Byron: *Childe Harold*, III, lxxvii, and Leslie Marchand, ed. *Byron's Letters and Journals*, 12 vols. (Cambridge, Mass.: Harvard University Press,

1973–1982), I, 171 and VII, 167: "That man was mad—and not well treated by his friends." Shelley on Rousseau, see "The Triumph of Life," ll. 241–243.

23. Rousseau, *Confessions* (New York: Black, n.d.), pp. 3, 5, 8, 55.

24. Byron, *Childe Harold*, III, lxxvii.

25. *Confessions*, p. 87.

III. ELEMENTS OF AUTOBIOGRAPHY

1. *Larousse Grand Dictionnaire*, 1866 edition, I, 979.

2. Coleridge letter of February, 1797, A. Turnbull, ed., *Biographia Epistolaris*, 2 vols. (London: Bell, 1911), I, 5.

3. Leslie Stephen, "Autobiography," *Cornhill*, 43 (1881), 410. If one could be dull, Stephen continues, "the very dulness would be interesting. . . . Also the autobiography may be more valuable in proportion to the amount of misrepresentation which it contains."

4. Carlyle, preface to *Wilhelm Meister*.

5. There have been many attempts in our time to define or describe autobiography as a genre. I have found the following especially useful or suggestive: Georges Gusdorf (see above, Chap. II, note 12); Wayne Shumaker, *English Autobiography* (Berkeley: University of California Press, 1954); Roy Pascal, *Design and Truth in Autobiography* (Cambridge, Mass.: Harvard University Press, 1960); John N. Morris, *Versions of the Self: Studies in English Autobiography from John Bunyan to John Stuart Mill* (New York: Basic Books, 1966); Jeffrey Mehlman, *A Structural Study of Autobiography* (Ithaca, N.Y.: Cornell University Press, 1974), limited to French writers; George P. Landow, ed., *Approaches* (see above, Chap. II, note 21), with Landow's admirable introduction; Robert F. Sayre, *The Examined Self* (Princeton, N.J.: Princeton University Press, 1964); Francis R. Hart, "Notes for an Anatomy of Modern Autobiography," *New Literary History*, 1 (1969–1970), 485–511; James Olney, ed., *Autobiography: Essays Theoretical and Critical*; and William C. Spengemann, *The Forms of Autobiography* (New Haven: Yale University Press, 1980), with an extensive critical bibliography, "The Study of Autobiography," pp. 170–245. Estelle C. Jelinek has edited, with a perceptive introduction, *Women's Autobiography: Essays in Criticism* (Bloomington, Ind.: Indiana University Press, 1980), fourteen essays, nearly all concerned with American women autobiographers (for the British counterparts are comparatively few—though Mitzi Myers, one of the contributors, offers an interesting discussion of Harriet Martineau). Avrom Fleishman's *Figures of Autobiography: The Language of Self-Writing in Victorian and Modern England* (Berkeley:

University of California Press, 1983), which treats many of the same nineteenth-century authors I have chosen to discuss, appeared too late for my present consideration. Fleishman's close study of "language" (typology, metaphor, myth, and symbol) differs, at all events, in purpose, method, and conclusions from my appraisal of similar sources.

6. Wilde's letters in the aggregate are consciously confessional; see Harry Wilson, "Epistolary Autobiography: The Letters of Oscar Wilde," *South Atlantic Quarterly*, 63 (1964), 406–413.

7. Isaac D'Israeli, "Some Observations," pp. 97–98.

8. R. H. Hutton, "John Stuart Mill's Autobiography," *Contemporary Thought and Thinkers*, 2 vols. (London: Macmillan, 1894), I, 181–182.

9. Tennyson, *In Memoriam*, sec. V, and Carlyle, *Sartor Resartus*, Book III, Chap. 3, and Book II, Chap. 10.

10. James Hogg, *Memoirs of the Author's Life*, Douglas S. Mack, ed. (New York: Barnes and Noble, 1972), p. 3.

11. *The Autobiography, Times, Opinions, and Contemporaries of Sir Egerton Brydges*, 2 vols. (London: Cochrane, 1834), I, 91–92, II, 363. This is a very early use of the word "autobiography" in a book title. Stephen Spender, "Confessions and Autobiography," *The Making of a Poem* (London: Hamish Hamilton, 1955), p. 65.

12. Beatrice Webb, *My Apprenticeship* (New York: Longmans Green, 1926), pp. 1, 250, 255.

13. A. J. C. Hare, *The Story of My Life*, 6 vols. (London: Allen, 1896–1900), I, v.

14. William Hazlitt, "On the Feeling of Immortality in Youth," *Complete Works*, 21 vols. (London: Dent, 1933), XVII, 199.

15. On Spencer, see Landow, *Approaches*, pp. xxx–xxxiv.

16. See Henry Green, *Pack My Bag: A Self-Portrait* (London: Hogarth, 1940), pp. 5–8.

17. Green, p. 14.

18. See De Quincey, "The Pains of Opium," *Confessions of an English Opium-Eater* (London: Cresset Press, 1950), pp. 328–329.

19. Herbert Read, "The Innocent Eye," *The Contrary Experience* (New York: Horizon, 1963), pp. 19–20, 55.

20. Russell, *Autobiography*, p. 250.

21. A. O. J. Cockshut, *Truth to Life: The Art of Biography in the Nineteenth Century* (New York: Harcourt Brace Jovanovich, 1976), p. 18.

22. Compton Mackenzie, *My Life and Times: Octave I, 1883–1891* (London: Chatto and Windus, 1963), p. 15.

23. Cf. Barbara Charlesworth Gelpi, "The Innocent I: Dickens' Influence on Victorian Autobiography," in Jerome H. Buckley, ed., *The*

Worlds of Victorian Fiction (Cambridge, Mass.: Harvard University Press, 1975), pp. 57–71.

24. Only "semi-fictional," since Butler transcribes many details directly from his memories of family life and reproduces his mother's actual letter as Christina's.

25. Jean François Marmontel, *Memoirs of Marmontel*, 4 vols. (London: Longman and Murray, 1805), I, 92. This translation of the *Mémoires* soon after its appearance in France may indicate a vogue in England for such writing, created by Rousseau's *Confessions*.

26. Cyril Connolly, *Enemies of Promise: Part III, A Georgian Childhood* (London: Routledge and Kegan Paul, 1949), p. 253. A. L. Rowse recalls another sort of education in *A Cornish Childhood* (New York: Macmillan, 1942), p. 5: "I hope that the book may reveal something of the inner process of a working-class child's education, and may have some value for the discussion as to the future shaping of our educational system."

27. See Evelyn Waugh, *A Little Learning* (London: Chapman and Hall, 1964), Graham Greene, *A Sort of Life* (London: The Bodley Head, 1971), and Henry Green, *Pack My Bag*, p. 236.

28. See Kenneth Clark, *Another Part of the Wood: A Self-Portrait* (London: Murray, 1974), p. 91. Clark calls the depression "*accidie, maladie des moines.*"

29. Erikson, *Identity*, pp. 19, 50.

30. Erikson, *Childhood and Society* (New York: Norton, 1963), p. 268.

31. Gerald Brennan, *A Life of One's Own*, 2 vols. (New York: Farrar Straus and Cudahy, 1962), II, 12.

32. Cf. Georges Gusdorf, "Conditions," p. 122, where he examines the act of confession and argues that to take cognizance of what has been changes what is.

33. Spender, *The Making of a Poem*, p. 66.

34. W. Hale White, *The Autobiography of Mark Rutherford* (New York: Cape and Smith, 1929), p. 190.

35. Goethe, "Selige Sehnsucht," from his *Westöstlicher Diwan*. The unsatisfied yearning or *Sehnsucht* is the central motif of C. S. Lewis's *Surprised by Joy*, discussed in my fourth chapter.

36. Russell, p. 220.

IV. AFTER *THE PRELUDE*

1. Quoted from Longfellow's *Journal* for August 21, 1850, by Jonathan Wordsworth, M. H. Abrams, and Stephen Gill, eds., *William Wordsworth: The Prelude, 1799, 1805, 1850* (New York: Norton, 1979), p. 561.

All quotations from *The Prelude* derive from this text; all are listed by the poem's book and line numbers in the 1850 version.

2. *The Prelude*, I, 637–647.

3. See anonymous notice, perhaps by David Masson, in *British Quarterly Review*, 12 (1850), 549–579, quoted in Norton edition, p. 556.

4. *Prelude*, XII, 253–258.

5. *Prelude* as "song": see esp. VI, 740, VIII, 477, XII, 8, XIV, 384–386. The present "song" in 1850 frequently replaces "I" (1805), as Wordsworth apparently tries to make the poem seem less egotistical; e.g., I, 630, II, 382, V, 538.

6. On books, see III, 581, and all of Book V.

7. Quotations in this paragraph, in order, VII, 477, III, 507–508, IV, 278, XII, 128–131, IV, 334–337.

8. IX, 73.

9. IX, 517–518.

10. See XII, 248–277.

11. VII, 643–649.

12. De Quincey on Wordsworth: see Edward Sackville-West, ed., *Confessions of an English Opium-Eater and Selections from the Autobiography* (London: Cresset Press, 1950), pp. 93, 97–98. Sackville-West prints the original 1822 text of the *Confessions*. See also the expanded 1856 *Confessions* (New York: Burt, n.d.), pp. 60–61, 79, 205, 214. Unless otherwise indicated, the notes that follow refer to the Sackville-West edition.

13. *Confessions*, p. 291.

14. *Prelude*, VI, 635, 639–640, and *Confessions*, pp. 22, 25 ("Autobiography"). De Quincey's "It was a wind that might have swept the fields of mortality" recalls "The winds come to me from the fields of sleep" from Wordsworth's Intimations Ode. De Quincey could have seen an unpublished manuscript of *The Prelude*, or he might well have heard Wordsworth's reading of the memorable lines on Simplon, eventually, in 1845, published as a separate unit.

15. De Quincey does not make it quite clear whether the "epiphany" occurred three times after the first occasion, or three times including the first.

16. On De Quincey's evasions and subterfuges, see Albert Goldman, *The Mine and the Mint: Sources for the Writings of Thomas De Quincey* (Carbondale, Ill.: Southern Illinois University Press, 1965).

17. The 1856 edition, p. 215n.

18. "To the Reader," *Confessions*, p. 253.

19. *Confessions*, p. 375.

20. P. 328.

21. P. 330. J. Hillis Miller makes an illuminating analysis of "the

Piranesi effect" in his chapter on De Quincey in *The Disappearance of God* (Cambridge, Mass.: Harvard University Press, 1963), pp. 67–69.

22. The 1856 edition, p. 188.

23. Spengemann (*Forms of Autobiography*, p. 230) speaks of "the transition from biographical to fictive metaphor enacted in the *Suspiria de Profundis*" as "the most significant movement in the whole history of autobiography."

24. *Confessions*, p. 306.

25. Nora Barlow, ed., *The Autobiography of Charles Darwin* (New York: Harcourt Brace, 1958), pp. 140–141.

26. Pp. 119, 109, 141.

27. *Origin*, italics mine; letter to Henry Fawcett, 1861, quoted by Barlow in appendix, p. 161, italics mine.

28. Darwin on Henslow et al., pp. 64, 100–103, 105.

29. P. 78.

30. P. 136.

31. Pp. 96–97. Darwin mentions only one child by name, Annie, who died at the age of ten. The memory of Annie brings a rare rush of tender emotion: "Tears still sometimes come into my eyes, when I think of her sweet ways." Howard Helsinger comments on the self-consciousness with which Darwin writes of his family and personal feelings: "Credence and Credibility: The Concern for Honesty in Victorian Autobiography," Landow, ed., *Approaches*, pp. 50–52.

32. P. 68.

33. P. 60. Darwin's cautious son, Francis, when editing the text, added a footnote to this passage: "I gather from some of my father's contemporaries that he has exaggerated the Bacchanalian nature of these parties."

34. Pp. 81, 82, 120–121.

35. Kenneth Clark, ed., John Ruskin, *Praeterita: Outlines of Scenes and Thoughts Perhaps Worthy of Memory in My Past Life* (London: Rupert Hart-Davis, 1949), pp. 42, 84, 85, 273.

36. *Praeterita*, pp. 250, 134, 139, 107.

37. *Praeterita*, pp. 210 (cf. 109), 330, 73, 189, 190.

38. *Praeterita*, pp. 119, 27, 169, 196, 183, 253.

39. *Praeterita*, pp. 79, 345.

40. See Elizabeth K. Helsinger, "The Structure of Ruskin's *Praeterita*," and Claudette Kemper Columbus, "Ruskin's *Praeterita* as Thanatography," in Landow, ed., *Approaches*, pp. 87–108, 109–127.

41. *Praeterita*, pp. 67, 109 (cf. 210), 488, 58, 337n., 222, 221.

42. Ruskin and Wordsworth: see Ruskin's essays of 1880–1881, *Fiction, Fair and Foul*, a negative view, but see also John D. Rosenberg, *The*

Darkening Glass (New York: Columbia University Press, 1961), pp. 5–6, 24, 94, for a number of interesting parallels.

43. *Praeterita*, pp. 104, 106, 281, 285, 206.

44. John Stuart Mill, "Bentham" (1838), in Edward Alexander, ed., *Literary Essays* (Indianapolis, Ind.: Bobbs-Merrill, 1967), p. 193.

45. I draw here on my own discussion of "the pattern of conversion" in *The Victorian Temper* (Cambridge, Mass.: Harvard University, 1951), pp. 87–108.

46. John Stuart Mill, *Autobiography* (New York: Columbia University Press, 1924), p. 113.

47. Carlyle, quoted by David Alec Wilson and David Wilson MacArthur, *Carlyle in Old Age* (New York: Dutton, 1934), p. 294.

48. *Autobiography*, p. 23.

49. *Autobiography*, p. 98.

50. Anne Mozley, ed., *Letters and Correspondence of John Henry Newman during His Life in the English Church*, 2 vols. (London: Longmans Green, 1890), I, 14n.

51. Mozley, I, 2, 92, 93, 64.

52. See Mozley, I, 132, where Newman makes the comparison with himself explicit. The riddle presents the snapdragon as speaker; see *Verses on Various Occasions* (London: Longmans Green, 1890), pp. 21–23. "Snapdragon" is dated October 2, 1827.

53. Newman, David De Laura, ed., *Apologia Pro Vita Sua* (New York: Norton, 1968), p. 13. This is the "definitive" 1886 edition.

54. *Apologia*, pp. 39–40.

55. *Apologia*, pp. 186, 187.

56. See Charles F. Harrold, *John Henry Newman* (New York: Longmans Green, 1945), p. 264, and Newman's comment in the *Apologia*, p. 84.

57. White, *Autobiography of Mark Rutherford*, p. 68.

58. *Rutherford*, pp. 67–68.

59. *Rutherford*, p. 224.

60. Russell, *Autobiography*, pp. 222, 316. This first volume, published in 1967, was followed in 1968 and 1969 by a second and third, bringing Russell's story from 1914 to 1967 but adding little to our estimate of his personality or his capacity as autobiographer.

61. *Autobiography*, p. 284.

62. C. S. Lewis, *Surprised by Joy* (London: Collins, 1959), pp. 20, 135, first published in 1935.

63. Cf. Lewis's comment, p. 135: "Wordsworth, I believe, made this mistake all his life. I am sure that all that sense of the loss of vanished

vision which fills *The Prelude* was itself vision of the same kind, if only he could have believed it."

64. *An Autobiography* (1954) extends and completes *The Story and the Fable* (1940); I quote from the Seabury Press edition of 1968. On Muir's poetry and values, see Daniel Hoffman, *Barbarous Knowledge: Myth in the Poetry of Yeats, Graves, and Muir* (New York: Oxford University Press, 1967), pp. 225–256.

65. *An Autobiography*, p. 14.

66. *An Autobiography*, p. 44.

67. *An Autobiography*, pp. 52, 193.

68. Muir speaks, p. 179, of his friend John Holms: "He held Traherne's and Vaughan's and Wordsworth's theory of childhood, which was bound up with his belief in immortality; in time he converted me to it, or rather made me realize that my own belief was the same as his."

69. *An Autobiography*, p. 170.

70. *An Autobiography*, p. 181.

V. INVENTED SELVES

1. William Butler Yeats, *Autobiographies* (London: Macmillan, 1973), pp. 469–470.

2. Letter to Lord Alfred Douglas, probably June, 1897, italics Wilde's, in Rupert Hart-Davis, ed., *The Letters of Oscar Wilde* (New York: Harcourt Brace and World, 1962), p. 590.

3. See above, Chap. IV.

4. *De Profundis*, the title applied to the long letter of January-March, 1897, *Letters*, p. 466. Jacques Barzun introduces a reprint of *De Profundis* (Vintage Books, 1964) with an acute assessment of Wilde's view of himself as a sort of tragic hero.

5. *Letters*, p. 466; see also p. 458, on the family name, and p. 500, where Wilde extols his own comedies above Congreve's.

6. *Letters*, p. 465.

7. *Letters*, p. 510.

8. *Letters*, p. 467; the last clause is quoted from *A Woman of No Importance*, Act IV.

9. *Letters*, p. 467.

10. *Letters*, pp. 458, 463.

11. *Letters*, p. 474; the last words here are quoted (not quite accurately) from *The Excursion*, IV, 139.

12. Quoted from a letter of April 17, 1898, from Robert Ross to Leonard Smithers, *Letters*, p. 730n.

13. George Moore, "Ave," *Hail and Farewell*, 2 vols. (New York: Appleton, 1925), I, 73, 75.

14. Susan Dick, ed., *Confessions of a Young Man* (Montreal: McGill-Queens University Press, 1972), p. 35.

15. Pp. 190, 231; the revised version dates from 1918.

16. P. 76.

17. P. 124.

18. See Dick, pp. 138, 228.

19. See William Irvine, ed., Edmund Gosse, *Father and Son* (Boston: Houghton Mifflin, 1965), p. xxxvii, and Evan Charteris, *The Life and Letters of Edmund Gosse* (New York: Harper, 1931), p. 307.

20. Gosse, p. 69.

21. P. 53.

22. P. 210.

23. Pp. 3, 4, 194.

24. P. 216.

25. P. 142.

26. P. 227.

27. *The Education of Henry Adams* (Boston: Houghton Mifflin, 1961), p. 307.

28. P. 68.

29. P. 4.

30. Pp. 4, 34, 56, 108, 140, 362.

31. P. 209.

32. P. 43.

33. Moore, quoted by Richard Ellmann, *James Joyce* (New York: Oxford University Press, 1965), p. 544. Ellmann also suggests that Gosse and Moore were possible influences on Joyce's *Portrait*, p. 153n. It is interesting to note that Gosse and Moore were among the select few to whom Joyce sent copies of the first edition of the novel; see Stuart Gilbert and Richard Ellmann, eds., *Letters of James Joyce*, 3 vols. (New York: Viking Press, 1966), II, 386.

VI. AUTOBIOGRAPHICAL FICTION

1. *Quarterly Review*, 24 (1821), 360–361. B. C. Southam identifies the reviewer as Richard Whately in *Jane Austen: The Critical Heritage* (London: Routledge and Kegan Paul, 1968), p. 87.

2. Jean Starobinski, "The Style of Autobiography," Olney, ed., *Autobiography*, p. 74.

3. V. S. Pritchett, *A Cab at the Door* (New York: Vintage Books, 1971), p. 207, first published in 1968.

4. Pritchett continues his story in *Midnight Oil* (1971), a chronicle of his years in France, Ireland, and Spain.

5. Wolfe, quoted by Harry Levin, *The Gates of Horn* (New York: Oxford University Press, 1966), p. 459.

6. Powell, in an interview, *New Yorker*, July 3, 1965, p. 17.

7. My comments on Gissing draw on my own essay, "A World of Literature: Gissing's *New Grub Street*," in Buckley, ed., *The Worlds of Victorian Fiction* (Cambridge, Mass.: Harvard University Press, 1975), pp. 223–234.

8. Green, quoted by John Updike, *New Yorker*, January 1, 1979, p. 62, from Green's *Pack My Bag*.

9. Patrick White, *Flaws in the Glass: A Self-Portrait* (New York: Viking, 1982), p. 20.

10. See Chap. II, n. 21, on Rousseau's impact, and Gordon Haight, *George Eliot* (New York: Oxford University Press, 1968), p. 65.

11. Dickens, letter of January 29, 1855, to Arthur Ryland, in Georgiana Hogarth and Mary Dickens, eds., *The Letters of Charles Dickens* (London: Macmillan, 1893), p. 355.

12. Cf. Gwendolyn Needham, "The Undisciplined Heart of David Copperfield," *Nineteenth-Century Fiction*, 9 (1954), 81–107.

13. Lawrence, letter of October 27, 1913, Harry T. Moore, ed., *The Collected Letters of D. H. Lawrence*, 2 vols. (New York: Viking Press, 1962), I, 234. My discussion of *Sons and Lovers* and Joyce's *Portrait* draws freely on my analysis of those novels in *Season of Youth* (Cambridge, Mass.: Harvard University Press, 1974), pp. 204–247.

14. Joyce, letter of October 31, 1925, to Damaso Alonso, *Letters*, III, 129.

15. Lawrence, "Return to Bestwood," Warren Roberts and Harry T. Moore, eds., *Phoenix II* (New York: Viking Press, 1968), pp. 257–266. The sketch was written in 1926.

16. Letter of August 22, 1912, *Letters*, II, 311.

17. William York Tindall, *A Reader's Guide to James Joyce* (New York: Noonday Press, 1959), p. 247.

18. See Robert Kiely, *Beyond Egotism: The Fiction of James Joyce, Virginia Woolf, and D. H. Lawrence* (Cambridge, Mass.: Harvard University Press, 1980).

19. Henry Miller, quoted from *New Republic*, May 18, 1938, by Steven G. Kellman, *The Self-Begetting Novel* (London: Macmillan, 1980), p. 122.

20. Gardner, "Afterword," in Robert A. Morace and Kathryn Van-

Spankeren, eds., *John Gardner: Critical Perspectives* (Carbondale, Ill.: Southern Illinois University Press, 1982), p. 149.

21. Kellman (note 19, above) gives the form extended analysis.

VII. POETRY AND THE PRINCIPLE OF SELF

1. Hallam Lord Tennyson, ed., *Alfred Lord Tennyson: A Memoir*, 2 vols. (New York: Macmillan, 1897), I, 305.

2. Arthur O. Prickard, *Autobiography* (London: Rivington, 1866), p. 21.

3. Leslie A. Marchand, ed., *Don Juan* (Boston: Houghton Mifflin, 1958), p. 3, Byron's 1819 preface.

4. A. Dwight Culler, ed., *Poetry and Criticism of Matthew Arnold* (Boston: Houghton Mifflin, 1961), p. 380, from Arnold's 1888 review of Edward Dowden's *Life of Shelley*.

5. Culler, pp. 208–209. Culler explains (p. 569) that the "modern critic," whom Arnold did not identify, was Goethe, who, in other contexts, appears as one of Arnold's modern heroes.

6. Lionel Trilling, more cautious than many other readers, nonetheless thought it "almost impossible not to find throughout 'Sohrab and Rustum' at least a shadowy personal significance"—*Matthew Arnold* (New York: Meriden Books, 1955), p. 124. Douglas Bush, on the other hand, rejected the notion of a possible subjective overtone—*Matthew Arnold* (New York: Macmillan, 1971), p. 69.

7. See Buckley, *Tennyson: The Growth of a Poet* (Cambridge, Mass.: Harvard University Press, 1960), p. 130.

8. The discussion of *In Memoriam* which follows draws in part, though with changes, on two of my earlier essays: "Victorian England: The Self-Conscious Society," in Josef L. Altholz, ed., *The Mind and Art of Victorian England* (Minneapolis, Minn.: University of Minnesota Press, 1976), pp. 7–12; and "The Persistence of Tennyson," in Richard A. Levine, ed., *The Victorian Experience: The Poets* (Athens, Ohio: Ohio University Press, 1982), esp. pp. 5–11.

9. Jacques Lacan, *The Language of the Self*, Anthony Wilden, trans. (Baltimore: Johns Hopkins University Press, 1968), pp. xiii, 160–161, 166, and Erikson, *Identity*, p. 108.

10. T. S. Eliot, *Essays Ancient and Modern* (London: Faber and Faber, 1936), p. 189. On Tennyson's use of personal detail, see Alan Sinfield, *The Language of Tennyson's In Memoriam* (New York: Barnes and Noble, 1971), p. 79.

11. "To—, After Reading a Life and Letters," Christopher Ricks, ed.,

The Poems of Tennyson (London: Longmans Green, 1969), p. 847. Ricks names several possible recipients, including Charles Tennyson Turner. I have suggested Charles in my *Tennyson*, p. 89.

12. Ricks, p. 1230.

13. Letter to Dante Gabriel Rossetti, January 1, 1877, William Michael Rossetti, ed., *Family Letters of Christina Rossetti* (New York: Scribner, 1908), p. 65.

14. See esp. the debated reading by Lona Mosk Packer, *Christina Rossetti* (Berkeley: University of California Press, 1963), pp. 149–151.

15. Cf. Constance W. Hassett, *The Elusive Self in the Poetry of Robert Browning* (Athens, Ohio: Ohio University Press, 1982), and Barbara Melchiori, *Browning's Poetry of Reticence* (Edinburgh: Oliver and Boyd, 1968).

16. See William Clyde De Vane, Jr., *A Browning Handbook* (New York: Crofts, 1940), pp. 349, 351–354. See also p. 356 on the relation of "House" to Rossetti's *House of Life*.

17. The Spanish poet's house even seems to anticipate Browning's house in Warwick Crescent, Paddington, the third house from a canal bridge, where Browning lived from 1861 till 1887.

18. Mill, quoted by De Vane, p. 41.

19. On autobiography in the *Parleyings*, see De Vane, *Browning's Parleyings: The Autobiography of a Mind* (New Haven: Yale University Press, 1927).

20. "Ego Dominus Tuus," *The Collected Poems of W. B. Yeats* (New York: Macmillan, 1942), p. 185.

21. E. M. W. Tillyard and C. S. Lewis, *The Personal Heresy* (London: Oxford University Press, 1939), p. 12.

22. W. H. Auden, "The Cave of Making," *About the House* (New York: Random House, 1965), p. 11. Quoted by permission of the publisher.

VIII. PERSONAL STATEMENTS

1. Quoted by Ian Hamilton, *Robert Lowell* (New York: Random House, 1982), p. 233.

2. "Confessional" poetry of this kind has been less conspicuous in England than in America. I therefore shift focus briefly to the American scene. The term, to which some of the poets themselves have objected, is used for rather indiscriminate praise by Robert Phillips, who tends to regard all subjective verse as literally autobiographical; see Phillips, *The Confessional Poets* (Carbondale, Ill.: Southern Illinois University Press, 1973).

3. Lowell and Tate, quoted by Hamilton, pp. 233, 237.

4. Louis Simpson, writing of Allen Ginsberg, Lowell, Dylan Thomas, and Sylvia Plath in his *A Revolution in Taste* (New York: Macmillan, 1978), denies that these four are really "confessional" poets or that they are unduly egocentric in their subjective concern; he prefers to think of them not as confessing private affairs so much as developing what he calls "the personal voice." David Kalstone takes a similar stand in *Five Temperaments* (New York: Oxford University Press, 1977), where he shows the aesthetic uses of personal materials in Lowell, Elizabeth Bishop, James Merrill, Adrienne Rich, and John Ashbery. Maxine Kumin, on the other hand, introducing the collected poems of Anne Sexton, gladly accepts the label: "Of all the confessional poets, none has quite Sexton's courage to make a clean breast of it" and "No other American poet has cried aloud publicly so many private details." See Anne Sexton, *The Complete Poems* (Boston: Houghton Mifflin, 1981), pp. xix, xxxiv.

5. Lowell, from "Unwanted" and "Epilogue," *Day by Day* (New York: Farrar, Straus and Giroux, 1977), pp. 121, 124, 127.

6. See R. D. Laing, *The Divided Self* (Chicago: Quadrangle Books, 1960), *The Politics of Experience* (New York: Pantheon Books, 1967), and *The Voice of Experience* (London: Lane, 1982). Reviewing the last of these, David Ingleby (*Times Literary Supplement*, September 3, 1982, p. 939) remarks: "Now, Laing's universe seems populated by monads, locked in their private worlds, with no means of communication except perhaps telepathy." On Laing, see also Andrew Collier, *R. D. Laing: The Philosophy and Politics of Psychotherapy* (Sussex, Eng.: Harvester Press, 1977). On schizophrenia in twentieth-century literature, drawing in part on Laing's theories, see John Vernon, *The Garden and the Map* (Urbana, Ill.: University of Illinois Press, 1973).

7. Adolf Wölfli was the subject of an exhibition, "The Art of the Insane," held from September 7 to October 21, 1978, at the Busch-Reisinger Museum, Cambridge, Mass. (and later in Chicago, Des Moines, and New York). I draw here on the catalogue and my own impressions of the exhibition.

8. Adrian Stokes, *Inside Out: An Essay in the Psychology and Aesthetic Appeal of Space* (London: Faber and Faber, 1947), pp. 24, 32. As evidence of continued interest in Stokes, I should cite the retrospective exhibition of his work at the Serpentine Gallery, London, in June 1982, sponsored by the Arts Council of Great Britain, and the publication of Stokes's collected poems, *With All the Views*, ed. Peter Robinson (Manchester: Carcanet, 1982). On Stokes, see John Pilling, *Autobiography and Imagination: Studies in Self-Scrutiny* (London: Routledge and Kegan Paul, 1981), pp. 133–143.

9. Dennis Proctor, ed., *The Autobiography of G. Lowes Dickinson* (London: Duckworth, 1973), p. 43.

10. Henry Miller, *Tropic of Cancer* (New York: Grove Press, 1961), p. 5. The novel first appeared in 1934. John O. Lyons (*Invention of the Self*, p. 219) uses the same sentence as a chapter epigraph.

11. Michel Leiris, *Manhood: A Journey from Childhood into the Fierce Order of Virility*, Richard Howard, trans. (New York: Grossman, 1963), pp. 3–4, 26, 42, 43, 122, 154. On Leiris, see also Pilling, pp. 63–80, and Susan Sontag's review of *Manhood* in her *Against Interpretation* (New York: Farrar, Straus and Giroux, 1966), p. 63, where the book is judged "obscene and repulsive," because "unredeemed by the slightest tinge of self-respect."

12. Samuel Beckett, *Company* (New York: Grove Press, 1981), pp. 61, 62–63. My epigraph for this chapter is quoted from p. 16.

13. *The Prelude*, XIII, 367–378. Karl J. Weintraub sees a similar desire for balance in Goethe as opposed to the sharply self-centered Rousseau; see Weintraub's excellent study, focused on the late eighteenth century, *The Value of the Individual: Self and Circumstance in Autobiography* (Chicago: University of Chicago Press, 1978), p. 379.

INDEX